Drunk Driving Defense

How to Beat the Rap

Attorney
Dennis A. Bjorklund

PRAETORIAN PUBLISHERS

This publication is intended to provide accurate and authoritative information about the subject matter covered. It is sold with the understanding that the publisher does not render legal, accounting or other professional services. If legal advice or other expert assistance is required, seek the legal services of a competent professional.

Persons using this publication when dealing with specific legal matters should exercise discretion and their own independent judgment, and research original sources of authority and local court rules and procedures.

The publisher and author make no representations concerning the contents of this publication and disclaim any warranties of merchantability or fitness for a particular purpose, or any other liability for reliance upon the contents container herein.

This publication is merely the commencement of dialogue with the readers, and we welcome suggestions to update the book for reprint and future editions. Send all comments to the address hereinbelow.

Library of Congress Cataloging-in-Publication Data
Bjorklund, Dennis A.
    Drunk Driving Defense: How to Beat the Rap.

    Includes index.
       1.   Drunk Driving--United States.   2.   Defense (Criminal procedure)--United States.   I.   Title.

First published in the United States of America in 1997
ISBN: 1-57502-986-3
Library of Congress Catalog Card Number: 98-68104
PRAETORIAN PUBLISHERS
P.O. Box 1847, Iowa City, Iowa 52240-1847

Printed in the United States by:
Morris Publishing * 3212 East Highway 30 * Kearney, NE 68847

CONTENTS

CHARTS

AUTHOR BIOGRAPHY

Dennis A. Bjorklund is an attorney specializing in drunk driving defense. He has written the only authoritative drunk driving books aimed at helping motorists protect their legal and constitutional rights against the unlawful infringement of law enforcement officers.

Drunk Driving Defense: How to Beat the Rap is a comprehensive synopsis at every phase of a drunk driving case, from the initial police stop through trial, with powerful insight into secret tactics used by law enforcement officers and prosecutors, and effective ways to avoid a conviction.

Drunk Driving: A Survival Guide for Motorists is a summary of the constitutional and statutory rights of motorists involved in a drunk driving case, including a thorough review of the drunk driving laws, criminal penalties, driver's license sanctions, and practical suggestions to avoid future legal problems.

Drunk Driving Laws: Rules of the Road When Crossing State Lines is a state by state overview of drunk driving laws, encompassing the legal standard for a criminal charge, penalties, driver's license sanctions, implied consent procedures, and chemical testing requirements.

Additional drunk driving-related books that were written specifically for motorists are scheduled for future release. *Drunk Driving and the Driver's License Suspension: How to Get Back on the Road* is intended to simplify the department of transportation bureaucracy so motorists can understand the administrative requirements and procedural aspects necessary to obtain a temporary restricted license (work permit), to calculate suspension periods, and achieve license reinstatement.

The Author has an extensive résumé of scholarly accomplishments, which include writing for the Iowa Law Review and being hand-selected as a distinguished literary contributor to author articles within his area of specialty.

PREFACE

Regardless of whether you experienced an arrest or were involved in a police stop where the officer suspected you of drunk driving, it is likely to occur in the near future. As drunk driving laws become more draconian and law enforcement personnel more extremist, it is only a matter of time before the net is cast over you or someone you know. The only way to protect yourself is to become knowledgeable about every aspect of drunk driving defense--laws, police procedure, scientific evidence, witness testimony, and trial strategy. Knowledge is power. This book offers essential information to elevate motorists to a superior position so they can protect and enforce their rights against overly intrusive police officers, zealous prosecutors, teetotaling counselors and prohibitionist judges.

There are numerous instances where drivers are wrongfully trapped in the legislature's broad and vaguely defined drunk driving laws. The presumption of intoxication at a statutorily prescribed blood-alcohol concentration is not necessarily applicable to every driver. In fact, motorists with higher tolerance levels can drive without exhibiting signs of impairment, but it is difficult and expensive to prove. More-over, politically correct juries of today often convict merely because the chemical test result exceeds the legal limit, rather than scientific explanations that refute the test's validity.

The most egregious circumstances involve innocent drivers who are forced to plead guilty to a drunk driving charge. The conviction could have been prevented if they knew how the system worked and were informed of their rights. Every motorist has the power to prevent a wrongful drunk driving charge. This text offers an overview of the drunk driving laws so motorists can understand their legal obligations, protect their legal rights, and avoid the consequences of a drunk driving conviction. Every effort was made to analyze the most common legal entanglements and present the material in an organized, straightforward, and illustrative manner.

The proposed strategies and recommendations, if properly followed and appropriately implemented, will enhance every motorist's opportunity to walk away from a drunk driving charge without the stigma of a criminal conviction. First and foremost, it is imperative to read the entire book from cover to cover. Each chapter offers legal strategies and helpful suggestions that make it difficult for law enforcement officials to arrest drunk drivers and hinders prosecuting attorneys from getting a conviction. The goal is to arm motorists with the necessary tools to make knowledgeable decisions about drinking and driving.

Drunk driving charges are won on the facts. Each case offers a unique legal and factual quandary that can significantly impact a jury verdict. Since this book offers extensive legal strategies to otherwise highly complex factual circumstances, it is impossible to provide definitive solutions to every legal issue. The goal is to provide general information regarding drunk driving laws, criminal procedure and various factors that influence a positive jury verdict. After thoroughly reviewing the contents, you will be in a better position to interview and select a qualified, competent lawyer.

When interviewing potential defense attorneys, be open and honest, and present all relevant facts. Even seemingly minor details can significantly impact the verdict. Withholding relevant facts or valuable evidence not only prevents defense attorneys from accurately analyzing the case to determine the likelihood of success, but also increases the chance for a conviction.

It is safe to assert that nothing can prevent a drunk driving *arrest*. Even sober drivers can be arrested for drunk driving. If there is no witness, the trial becomes simply the driver's word against the officer's. If the officer testifies to observing bloodshot and watery eyes, flushed face, and rambling speech, this is sufficient for a conviction, despite the absence of hard evidence to prove alcohol was consumed.

It may seem preposterous to the average American, but some police officers overstep the ethical boundaries for a variety of reasons, such as quotas, increasing their conviction rate, or personal inclinations. To combat this prejudice, it is essential for motorists to know their rights so they can avoid a wrongful drunk driving charge.

Unfortunately, asserting your legal rights has consequences. It often requires a trial, which entails legal defense costs, an extensive time commitment, and a nerve-racking experience. However, this is nothing compared to the cost of a criminal conviction--statutory fines, incarceration, probation, increased insurance rates, driver's license suspension, limited employment opportunities, ignition interlock devices, vehicle impoundment or immobilization, and the risk of a second offense drunk driving charge.

When reviewing the chapters, always remember that the legal climate is extremely volatile in this area. State legislatures are constantly changing the drunk driving laws, and the courts are continuously redefining the parameters of police authority and motorists' rights. Since many recently adopted laws and important constitutional issues have yet to be addressed by the courts, there is no definitive legal precedent to offer absolute strategies. Thus, the proffered strategies and suggestions are legal interpretations of the law or predictions about future tendencies in the judiciary. To receive the most up-to-date advice about the rapidly changing laws, always consult an attorney who specializes in drunk driving defense. Most attorneys have a general understanding of the laws, but few thoroughly compre-hend the critical legal issues, statutory changes, impact on driving privileges, or most recent trends in criminal defense.

By understanding and enforcing individual constitutional rights, innocent drivers can prevent a wrongful conviction and avoid becoming another casualty in the war against drunk driving.

1

Drunk Driving Laws

State lawmakers presume motorists do not realize the dangers and consequences of drinking and driving. Consequently, they enact laws designed to protect society and attain several positive results. Since it is political suicide to resist harsher drunk driving laws, every year the legislature increases the criminal penalties and driver's license sanctions. In some states, convicted drunk drivers must attend drunk driving classes or reality-based substance abuse classes as a form of rehabilitation to deter future offenses.

Most drunk driving statutes require the prosecution to prove that the motorist is either operating a motor vehicle while under the influence of an alcoholic beverage or drug, or has a blood-alcohol concentration (BAC) at or above the legal limit, usually .08 or .10. "Under the influence" is often defined as a motorist exhibiting one or more of the following characteristics: 1) affected reason or mental ability; 2) impaired judgment; 3) visibly excited emotions; or 4) losing control of bodily actions or motions so that the ability to safely operate a motor vehicle is diminished to any extent.

Punishment and Sanctions

Drunk driving laws have a twofold system of deterrence: criminal (jail and fines) and civil (driver's license suspension). The criminal penalty escalates with each offense and any aggravating circumstance, such as damage to property, serious personal injury, or death. The civil sanction is based upon similar factors, as well as evidence of a chemical test refusal and the defendant's driving history.

With respect to minors, drunk driving laws are often less tolerant of underage drinking and driving. Many states have imposed harsher criminal and civil penalties. Although the criminal punishment is often the same, a civil sanction can usually occur with a lower BAC level, and there is a lengthier driver's license suspension.

Criminal Punishment

The severity of criminal punishment is primarily based upon the number of prior drunk driving convictions. The level of offense is usually determined by the number of years between conviction and date of offense, regardless of whether a deferred judgment was received. Most states count all prior drunk driving offenses, regardless of whether it occurred in a different state (provided the statute is comparable). The number of years used to enhance the criminal penalty varies from state to state, so purchase a copy of *Drunk Driving Laws: Rules of the Road When Crossing State Lines* to confirm the laws in your jurisdiction. For instance, Alabama and Arizona have a 5-year penalty enhancement period, whereas the District of Columbia enhances the offense up to 15 years after a drunk driving conviction.

When calculating the level of offense, consider the following illustration according to Iowa's 12-year enhancement statute. If convicted on January 1, 1998 and accused of drunk driving on December 31, 2009, the motorist will be charged with second offense drunk driving (even if the conviction does not go on record until July 1, 2010). The period of enhancement is measured from the date of conviction to the date of the next alleged criminal act.

In another scenario involving Iowa law, if a motorist is convicted on January 1, 1998, convicted on January 1, 2005, and accused of drunk driving on January 2, 2010, the motorist will be charged with second offense drunk driving. It is not a third offense because more than 12 years lapsed between the date of the first conviction and the date of the alleged third drunk driving incident (i.e., 12 years and one day).

Moreover, the severity of imprisonment and fines varies from state to state. It is essential to purchase a copy of *Drunk Driving Laws: Rules of the Road When Crossing State Lines* to confirm the statutory punishment in your jurisdiction. There can be a grave disparity between jurisdictions, so know your rights (and the consequences) in advance.

First Offense. A first offense drunk driving conviction can vary significantly from state to state. Many states have a minimum number of hours in jail and a standard fine. There is also a discretionary range of punishment for the judge to consider, which includes a maximum jail sentence and loftier fine. Some jurisdictions allow the fine to be waived if there is no injury to person or property, or the court can grant a deferred judgment to remove the conviction from the defendant's criminal record.

In some jurisdictions there are numerous restrictions when attempting to receive a deferred judgment. For instance, Iowa law prohibits a deferred judgment or suspended sentence under the following circumstances: 1) BAC .151 or more; 2) chemical test refusal; 3) bodily injury, serious injury or death to others; or 4) a prior drunk driving conviction or deferred judgment.

In lieu of a fine, the court can order unpaid community service. If a jail sentence is imposed, the court is often empowered to accommodate the defendant's work schedule, e.g., order work release or allow the sentence to be served on weekends.

A substance abuse evaluation is usually required prior to sentencing and the court typically orders the motorist to attend a drunk driving class, while other defendants may be required to participate in a reality-based substance abuse education program.

Second Offense. A second offense drunk driving conviction has a longer mandatory jail sentence and higher minimum fine. Some jurisdictions require the jail term to be served on consecutive days unless undue hardship exists. There is also a discretionary range of punishment for the judge to consider with a maximum jail sentence (usually one year) and a significant fine. In some jurisdictions a deferred judgment or suspended sentence is still available.

Comparable to a first offense drunk driving, a substance abuse evaluation is usually required, and in lieu of a fine, the court can order unpaid community service.

Third or Subsequent Offense. A third or subsequent drunk driving offense usually results in a felony conviction ranging from a minimum sentence (usually 30 days in jail) and fine, to a maximum sentence of imprisonment (approximately two years) and excessive fine. In some jurisdictions, the jail sentence must be served on consecutive days unless the defendant can show undue hardship.

In lieu of a fine, the court can order unpaid community service. Usually a substance abuse evaluation is required prior to sentencing and most defendants must undergo appropriate treatment in a residential treatment facility.

Serious Injury to Others. If the drunk driving incident results in serious injury to others, the maximum punishment is usually five years in prison, and the defendant is not entitled to a deferred judgment.

Death to Others. If the drunk driving incident results in a death, the maximum punishment can be 25 years in prison. In most circumstances, the defendant is not entitled to a deferred judgment.

Penalties for Minors. Persons under the age of 21 are subject to the same laws as motorists who have reached the age of majority with one major exception: minors will suffer a driver's license suspension with a BAC as low as .02, and more severe penalties if the BAC result is over the legal limit.

Substance Abuse Requirements

Following a drunk driving arrest, the court may order the defendant to obtain a substance abuse evaluation. Although the law usually requires that upon *conviction*, the court may order a substance abuse evaluation and appropriate treatment, many judges require an evaluation within ten days of the initial appearance.

First Offense. Upon conviction for first offense drunk driving, many jurisdictions require the defendant to attend and pay for a drunk driving course. Moreover, proof of completion is often required by the department of transportation before driving privileges will be reinstated. If the BAC is at least twice the legal limit, the court usually orders a substance abuse evaluation and mandates completion of all recommended treatment.

Second Offense. Upon conviction for second offense drunk driving, the court usually requires a substance abuse evaluation and the completion of all recommended treatment. If the recommendation includes commitment to a substance abuse treatment facility, the defendant will receive credit for time served. Although the court can specify the length of stay, it frequently relies upon the recommendation of the evaluating facility to determine when the defendant has received the maximum benefit from treatment.

Third or Subsequent Offense. Although some states specify punishment for individual offenses beyond the third, most jurisdictions offer the same punishment for all subsequent offenses. Upon conviction for a third or subsequent offense drunk driving, the substance abuse requirements are typically the same as second offense drunk driving. The defendant must undergo an evaluation, complete all recommended treatment, and often receives credit for time served in a treatment facility.

Additional Substance Abuse Treatment. In addition to substance abuse classes or treatment, the court can order probation and post-treatment substance abuse services. Failure to comply with the court order can result in contempt of court charges, performing unpaid community service, or an additional probationary period.

Paying for Treatment. If court-ordered treatment is too costly and the defendant qualifies as an indigent, the state will often pay for the expense. Similarly, if the court requires inpatient substance abuse treatment, the state typically pays the cost for financially impoverished defendants.

Drunk Driving Course. In addition to treatment, the defendant is often required to enroll, attend and pay for a state authorized drunk driving course. A person will not be denied enrollment because of income. If the defendant qualifies as an indigent, the state frequently pays most of the expense.

For persons between the ages of 16 and 21, some jurisdictions require enrollment in a reality-based education program to prevent future substance abuse related law violations. The program includes supervised tours of hospitals, treatment facilities or morgues.

Restitution

The court generally orders the defendant to pay restitution to victims, which is credited toward any future civil judgment. Evidence in a restitution proceeding is not admissible in a subsequent civil trial. The prosecuting attorney is often required to file a statement of pecuniary damages within 30 days of sentencing to outline restitution costs.

Driver's License Sanction

Most states predicate their motor vehicle licensure laws on one simple legal concept--driving is a privilege, not a fundamental right--so any driver's license sanction is remedial, not punitive. Consequently, a drunk driving criminal charge is separate and distinct from a driver's license suspension. For example, despite an acquittal on a drunk driving charge, the department of transportation is still allowed to suspend driving privileges for a drunk driving offense. The rationale is twofold.

First, there is a legal distinction surrounding the definition of punishment. A criminal charge is considered punishment because a jail sentence can be imposed, while a driver's license suspension is remedial because no incarceration can result. Second, there is a different standard of proof. In a criminal case, the state must prove guilt beyond a reasonable doubt, whereas a civil case only requires a preponderance of the evidence (i.e., more likely than not). Despite the cockeyed rationale, this remains the predominate judicial interpretation of drunk driving laws.

Notice of Suspension

The driver's license suspension period typically begins ten days after receiving notice of the suspension, either by certified mail from the department of transportation or verbally from the officer at the time of the chemical test failure or refusal. The officer will usually serve notice, confiscate the driver's license, issue a 10-day permit, and forward the license to the department of transportation. This allows the motorist sufficient time to file an appeal to challenge the legitimacy of the suspension.

Driver's License Suspension Hearing

In most driver's license suspension hearings, the motorist must contest the sanction by requesting a hearing within ten days of receiving notice of suspension. The hearing is held by an administrative law judge (ALJ) who determines whether the officer had reasonable grounds to believe the motorist was operating a vehicle in violation of the drunk driving laws. The ALJ will either rescind or sustain the suspension. The motorist can appeal the decision to the director of driver services, who will rescind or sustain the suspension, or order a new hearing. Usually the motorist is allowed to drive during the pendency of the hearing or appeal; however, this does not always apply to minors.

If new evidence is subsequently discovered that would warrant cancellation of the suspension, or the trial court rules that the officer did not have probable cause to request a chemical test, or the test was held inadmissible or invalid, a petition to reopen the hearing may be filed. In addition, if the department of transportation fails to abide by statutorily prescribed deadlines, the suspension is usually rescinded.

License Suspension Period

The driver's license suspension is based primarily upon the number of prior drunk driving incidents and the implied consent law. The length of suspension is determined by various factors, such as the defendant's age, the number of years between the prior conviction and date of the most recent offense (regardless of whether a deferred judgment was received), and driving history (including the amount and severity of other offenses). As indicated, each jurisdiction has a different time frame to enhance the level of offense, so purchase *Drunk Driving Laws: Rules of the Road When Crossing State Lines* for an overview of every state's drunk driving laws.

A first offense drunk driving conviction usually has a license suspension, reinstatement fee, and a hard suspension where no temporary restricted license (TRL) is available. Another important characteristic of the drunk driving laws is an enhanced driver's license suspension based upon the presence or absence of a chemical test. Furthermore, some states have longer suspension periods for minors, and zero tolerance laws that impose a driver's license sanction when their BAC is .02 or more.

Serious Injury to Others. If the motorist is involved in a personal injury accident, the court usually determines whether the consumption of alcohol resulted in serious injury to anyone other than the driver. If so, the court can often suspend driving privileges for one year, in addition to any other suspension, and no TRL is issued until the minimum period of ineligibility has expired.

Death to Others. When an accident results in a death, which was caused by the motorist's drunken driving, in some states the court can suspend driving privileges for six years with no TRL for at least two years. In addition, the defendant is often required to attend a drunk driving course, obtain a substance abuse evaluation, and complete all recommended treatment.

Driving Under Suspension. Operating a motor vehicle while driving privileges are suspended because of a drunk driving charge is a criminal offense and the defendant will have an additional suspension period and lose all TRL privileges.

Temporary Restricted License (TRL)

Generally, in a drunk driving incident the motorist remains eligible for a TRL, either through the department of transportation or by court order. However, the TRL is only authorized for certain limited uses, and the defendant is often required to install an ignition interlock device in all vehicles. A TRL will not be issued for at least two years if a drunk driving incident resulted in a death.

Minors. A minor is often ineligible for a TRL when the license suspension is the result of a drunk driving offense.

Commercial License. Motorists possessing a commercial vehicle license are eligible for a TRL, provided the drunk driving incident did not involve the operation of a commercial vehicle.

Authorized Uses. A TRL can only be used to travel from home to specified places that are verifiable by the department of transportation. Appropriate uses include: Full or part-time employment; continuing health care of self or dependent persons; continuing education while pursuing a diploma, degree or certification; substance abuse treatment; or court-ordered community service. A TRL cannot be used for pleasure driving.

Eligibility Requirements. Before an applicant is eligible for a TRL, most states have statutory requirements that must be satisfied: 1) the applicant has only one prior drunk driving suspension within the penalty enhancement period; 2) their license is not under suspension for any other reason; and 3) the hard suspension period has elapsed.

Bus Drivers. A TRL does not allow a person to operate a school bus.

Ignition Interlock Device

Upon conviction, many jurisdictions require the installation of an ignition interlock device (IID) in all vehicles operated by the defendant. The IID is a mechanism connected to the vehicle's ignition to measure ethanol within a person's breath. When a driver blows into the device and the ethanol level exceeds a pre-programmed BAC result, the vehicle's ignition will not function. Some IIDs require constant monitoring of breath-ethanol levels, even while the vehicle is operating.

The period of installation usually parallels the length of a driver's license suspension, though it can extend up to the maximum term of incarceration allowed by statute. The IID is often required for a temporary restricted license. Failure to install the device within a reasonable time period can result in contempt of court, and tampering with the device is a criminal offense punishable by jail or fine.

Reinstatement of License

After driving privileges are suspended, the defendant is usually required to attend a state-approved drunk driving course. In some jurisdictions, the defendant is required to obtain a substance abuse evaluation, treatment, or rehabilitation services. There is no reinstatement of driving privileges until the defendant shows proof of completion to the department of transportation, and fulfills other financial obligations, such as a reinstatement fee.

Vehicle Impoundment/Immobilization

Impoundment is where the police take physical possession of a motor vehicle and store it on state property. The vehicle owner must pay a storage fee for the duration of the impoundment order. Immobilization is where the police render the vehicle inoperable, often by installing a club on the steering wheel, and store it on the owner's property. Immobilization is considerably less expensive than impoundment; however, the judge has discretion to impose either sanction.

First Offense. There is usually no impoundment or immobilization issue for first offense drunk driving convictions.

Second or Subsequent Offense. At the sentencing hearing, the court will order impoundment or immobilization of the vehicle that was involved in the drunk driving offense. The vehicle is not released until the period of impoundment or immobilization expires--typically the same length of time as the driver's license suspension--and all fees and costs are paid. Operating or selling a vehicle subject to an impoundment or immobilization order is a criminal offense, resulting in vehicle seizure and forfeiture. Similarly, when the owner of an impounded or immobilized vehicle unlawfully allows the defendant to drive, the owner is subject to criminal charges and joint civil liability for any resulting damages.

There are usually two exceptions to the impoundment or immobilization law. First, if the vehicle title is transferred into the name of a third party prior to the sentencing hearing, the law does not apply. The court cannot order impoundment or immobilization if the vehicle is no longer owned by someone directly associated with the drunk driving incident. *Strategy:* Transfer the vehicle title prior to sentencing to avoid the problems affiliated with impoundment or immobilization issues.

Second, the law allows a person to drive an impounded or immobilized vehicle, but only under limited circumstances. It usually requires a court order, proof that the applicant's driving privilege is not suspended, and installation of an ignition interlock device. Only a limited class of persons are eligible, e.g., joint owners who are not immediate family members, or family members in a 1-vehicle household.

2

Legal Definitions

In many jurisdictions the term "drunk driving" is a misnomer because a person does not have to drink or drive to be convicted of drunk driving. For whatever reason, the legal system has curtailed motorists' rights to make it is easier for prosecutors to obtain a conviction. The double standard of judicial precedent that applies to drunk driving cases versus all other criminal charges is one of the most frustrating aspects of legal defense. Consequently, there are numerous instances where persons are wrongfully convicted of a serious criminal offense even though there was no proof of drinking or driving.

This chapter will provide motorists with the necessary information and knowledge to prevent a wrongful conviction. Innocent motorists must know their rights to avoid becoming victims of these erroneously interpreted and unjustly enforced laws.

Legal Definition of Driving

The first legal injustice is that actual physical control of a motor vehicle is not always necessary for a drunk driving conviction. To constitute driving, there is usually a requirement that the driver have sufficient control over the vehicle. Of course, based upon recent interpretations of the law, this is not difficult to prove.

In one case, a motorist and his friend drove into a ditch, burying the car in mud. While making a futile attempt to dislodge the car, an officer arrived and charged the person behind the wheel with drunk driving. Although the vehicle was inoperable and there was no proof the person behind the wheel actually drove the car into the ditch, the court senselessly upheld the conviction claiming the driver had sufficient control of the vehicle.

Engine Running. Many courts believe that a running engine is sufficient control to constitute driving. Similar to the prior illustration, a motorist drove into a ditch, down a steep embankment, and immobilized the van in 18" of snow. It was impossible to move the vehicle, let alone drive it. The driver walked for help while the passenger stayed with the vehicle. Since it was subzero temperatures, the passenger occasionally started the engine to remain warm. When the officer arrived, the passenger was in the driver's seat with the motor running, and was charged with drunk driving.

Currently, it is not considered driving if the keys are in the ignition and the engine is turned off. However, if the person is sitting in the passenger seat while the engine is running, a drunk driving charge could be filed. Absent corroborating witnesses or someone accepting responsibility as the driver, the passenger would technically satisfy the legal definition of driving.

Informant Reports. With the advent of cellular telephones, it is increasingly common for motorists to notify police of a possible drunk driver. In one case, a client was returning home on the interstate when a motorist used a cellular phone to notify state police of a potential drunk driver. An officer waited for the suspect to approach, observed her driving behavior, and then initiated a drunk driving arrest. In another case, a resentful bank teller contacted the police to report an irate customer as a potential drunk driver. An officer observed the car, initiated a stop, and charged the motorist with drunk driving.

Although informants are an important source for detecting drunk drivers, officers cannot rely solely upon the informant's report to stop an alleged drunken driver. Instead, the officer must personally observe the driving behavior before instituting a vehicle stop. Typically, the informant is an unknown motorist with no connection to the driver or police department; however, if the informant is more reliable and was used by the police in the past, the officer may not need to observe the driving behavior before initiating a police stop. Irrespective of the legal technicalities, an unscrupulous officer can easily fabricate a traffic law violation to justify the police stop.

Witness Evidence. Another drunk driving scenario involves the legal impact of not having corroborating evidence to substantiate the motorist's version of the events. The best corroboration is eyewitness testimony or videotape recordings. For instance, in one case an officer arrived on the scene of a one-car accident accompanied by cameramen from the television show "Real Stories of the Highway Patrol." The officer adamantly contended that the driver was intoxicated, but the videotape convinced the jury that the defendant was sober. Ironically, the videotape also showed the officer following a possible drunk driver, but he opted for a high profile arrest. Absent this videotape, the defendant could have been wrongfully convicted of drunk driving. Unfortunately, many innocent drivers will be convicted because they lack corroborating evidence to prove their innocence.

Although corroborating evidence is sometimes helpful, it can also be harmful. In another case, a vehicle passenger knew devastating information about the driver. He was a good friend of the defendant, and willingly admitted that the driver consumed a 12-pack of beer in three hours. Needless to say, the passenger was excluded from the defense witness list. The prosecutor was aware of the witness but assumed the testimony would be favorable to the defense, so he never contacted the witness to request a statement. By excluding this damning testimony, the defendant was acquitted.

Other potentially useful witnesses include a cell mate, bondsman, anyone who saw the defendant shortly after the arrest, as well as acquaintances who saw the defendant approximately one hour prior to the arrest. If the defendant was given a telephone call, the recipient should be questioned. Often an attorney is contacted, and if the evidence is favorable, this can be highly persuasive testimony at trial. The attorney would represent an unbiased witness, and could rebut the officer's allegation of slurred, thick or incomprehensible speech, as well as rambling or lethargic dialogue.

Placing the Defendant at the Scene. In certain circumstances, the prosecution must place the defendant at the scene, and often behind the wheel, to prove the "driving" element of a drunk driving offense. For example, in an accident where the bodies are thrown from a car or the driver leaves the scene before police arrive, it can be difficult to prove the defendant was driving. Even if the driver volunteers incriminating information, the prosecution must provide independent, circumstantial evidence of driving. Thus, it is important to attack eyewitness accounts or other evidence that could establish the defendant was driving.

As previously indicated, there are possible scenarios where a motorist can escape a drunk driving charge using legal technicalities; however, proving the driving element of the crime is usually uncomplicated. Current drunk driving laws make it nearly impossible to disprove driving, especially if the defendant is the sole occupant of a vehicle or lacks corroborating evidence. Although drunk driving charges may be filed, obtaining a conviction is an entirely different matter.

Legal Definition of Drunk

In addition to driving, the prosecution must prove the motorist was "intoxicated" at the time of driving. Most states presume a motorist is legally intoxicated if their BAC is .10 or more (.08 in 16 states). Moreover, the statutes often incorporate drugs and medication into the definition of drunk, so criminal charges can be filed for using legal or illegal substances.

By comparing body weight to alcohol consumption, motorists can reasonably predict BAC levels to avoid driving while intoxicated. (*See* Charts 2 and 3). Of course, many factors affect BAC levels--biological composition, individual metabolism, and alcohol absorption rates--so the charts only offer a general guideline for responsible drinking. Thus, it is always best to drink less than the amount indicated for your particular weight.

Factors Affecting BAC Levels

Ingested alcohol absorbs at a slower pace in the stomach than the small intestine. The length of time alcohol remains in the stomach depends on the beverage consumed, presence of food, biological factors and stress. When alcohol lingers in the stomach, intoxication is less likely to occur because the enzymes and bacteria continuously metabolize alcohol before it is absorbed into the bloodstream.

Chart 1

Alcohol Content of Common Beverages

Beverage Type	% of Alcohol by Volume	Typical Serving Size	Amt. of Alcohol/ Typical Serving
Regular Beer	5 percent	12 ounces	.60 ounces
Light Beer	4 percent	12 ounces	.48 ounces
Table Wine	12 percent	5 ounces	.60 ounces
Wine Cooler	5 percent	12 ounces	.60 ounces
Hard Liquor*	40 percent	1 ¼ ounces	.50 ounces

Note: Approximate alcohol content in typical servings of common alcoholic beverages. The figures shown are averages for all brands. The actual amount of alcohol in any type of drink varies somewhat from brand to brand.

* Hard liquor represents common brands of vodka, gin, rum, tequila, bourbon, and scotch. Certain name brands may have a higher alcohol content.

Alcohol Content. There are numerous factors that affect BAC levels. The most obvious is alcohol potency. To calculate the percentage of alcohol, divide the alcohol proof by 2. Many people underestimate BAC levels because they consume beverages with a higher alcohol content. Charts 2 and 3 estimate BAC levels based upon typical alcoholic beverages: 12-ounce domestic beer, 4-ounce glass of wine, or 1 ¼-ounce shot of 80 proof alcohol. (*See* Chart 1).

Alcohol Ingested. Another distortion is the amount of alcohol in a drink, especially mixed drinks, which frequently contain more than one shot of booze. In addition, the size of the drink can affect estimated BAC levels. Using mugs of beer, a large wine glass, or an oversized shot glass can mislead drinkers into consuming more alcohol than expected.

Food Consumption. When estimating BAC levels, consider the amount of food consumed and the time between eating and drinking. This will impact the speed at which alcohol is absorbed into the bloodstream. Alcohol consumed during or after a meal will absorb into the bloodstream at a slower pace; conversely, drinking on an empty stomach leads to rapid alcohol absorption.

Chart 2: Men's BAC Levels Based on Body Weight (pounds) and Hours of Drinking

lbs.:	120				140				160				180				200				220				240			
DRINKS / hrs.:	1	2	3	4	1	2	3	4	1	2	3	4	1	2	3	4	1	2	3	4	1	2	3	4	1	2	3	4
1	.02	.00	--	--	.01	.00	--	--	.01	.00	--	--	.00	.00	--	--	.00	.00	--	--	.00	.00	--	--	.00	.00	--	--
2	.05	.03	.01	.00	.04	.02	.00	.00	.03	.01	.00	.00	.02	.01	.00	.00	.02	.00	.00	.00	.02	.00	.00	.00	.01	.00	.00	.00
3	.08	.06	.05	.03	.06	.05	.03	.01	.05	.04	.02	.01	.04	.03	.01	.00	.04	.02	.01	.00	.04	.02	.00	.00	.03	.01	.00	.00
4	.11	.09	.08	.06	.09	.07	.06	.04	.08	.06	.04	.03	.06	.05	.03	.02	.06	.04	.02	.01	.05	.04	.02	.00	.04	.03	.01	.00
5	.14	.12	.11	.09	.11	.10	.08	.07	.10	.08	.07	.05	.08	.07	.06	.04	.07	.06	.04	.03	.07	.05	.04	.02	.06	.04	.03	.01
6	.17	.15	.14	.12	.14	.11	.11	.09	.12	.11	.09	.07	.10	.09	.07	.06	.09	.08	.06	.04	.09	.07	.05	.04	.07	.06	.05	.03
7	.20	.19	.17	.15	.17	.15	.13	.12	.15	.13	.11	.10	.12	.11	.09	.08	.11	.09	.08	.06	.10	.09	.07	.06	.09	.07	.06	.04
8	.23	.22	.20	.18	.19	.18	.16	.14	.17	.15	.14	.12	.14	.13	.11	.10	.13	.11	.10	.08	.12	.10	.09	.07	.10	.09	.07	.06
9	.26	.25	.23	.22	.22	.20	.19	.17	.19	.18	.16	.14	.16	.15	.13	.12	.15	.13	.11	.10	.14	.12	.11	.09	.12	.10	.09	.07
10	.29	.28	.26	.25	.24	.23	.21	.20	.21	.20	.18	.17	.18	.17	.15	.14	.16	.15	.13	.12	.15	.14	.12	.11	.13	.12	.10	.09
11	.33	.31	.29	.28	.27	.25	.24	.22	.24	.22	.21	.19	.20	.19	.17	.16	.18	.17	.15	.13	.17	.16	.14	.12	.15	.13	.12	.10
12	.36	.34	.32	.31	.30	.28	.26	.25	.26	.24	.23	.21	.22	.21	.19	.18	.20	.18	.17	.15	.19	.17	.16	.14	.16	.15	.13	.12
13	--	--	.36	.34	--	--	.29	.27	--	--	.25	.24	--	--	.21	.20	--	--	.19	.17	--	--	.17	.16	--	--	.15	.13
14	--	--	.39	.37	--	--	.32	.30	--	--	.27	.26	--	--	.23	.22	--	--	.20	.19	--	--	.19	.17	--	--	.16	.15
15	--	--	--	.40	--	--	--	.33	--	--	--	.28	--	--	--	.24	--	--	--	.21	--	--	--	.19	--	--	--	.16
16	--	--	--	.43	--	--	--	.35	--	--	--	.30	--	--	--	.26	--	--	--	.22	--	--	--	.24	--	--	--	.18

Chart 3: Women's BAC Levels Based on Body Weight (pounds) and Hours of Drinking

lbs.:	100				120				140				160				180				200				220			
hrs.:	1	2	3	4	1	2	3	4	1	2	3	4	1	2	3	4	1	2	3	4	1	2	3	4	1	2	3	4
D 1	.03	.01	---	---	.02	.01	---	---	.02	.00	---	---	.01	.00	---	---	.01	.00	---	---	.01	.00	---	---	.00	.00	---	---
R 2	.07	.06	.04	.03	.06	.04	.03	.01	.05	.03	.02	.00	.04	.02	.01	.00	.03	.02	.02	.00	.03	.01	.00	.00	.02	.01	.00	.00
I 3	.12	.10	.09	.07	.10	.08	.06	.05	.08	.06	.05	.03	.07	.05	.04	.02	.06	.04	.03	.01	.05	.03	.02	.00	.04	.03	.01	.00
N 4	.16	.15	.13	.12	.13	.12	.10	.08	.11	.10	.08	.06	.10	.08	.06	.05	.08	.07	.05	.04	.07	.06	.04	.02	.06	.05	.03	.02
K 5	.21	.19	.18	.16	.17	.15	.14	.12	.14	.13	.11	.10	.12	.11	.09	.08	.11	.09	.08	.06	.09	.08	.06	.05	.08	.07	.05	.04
S 6	.25	.24	.22	.21	.21	.19	.17	.16	.18	.16	.14	.13	.15	.14	.12	.10	.13	.12	.10	.09	.12	.10	.08	.07	.10	.09	.07	.06
7	.30	.28	.27	.25	.24	.22	.21	.20	.21	.19	.18	.16	.18	.16	.15	.13	.16	.14	.13	.11	.14	.12	.11	.09	.12	.11	.09	.08
8	.34	.33	.31	.30	.28	.26	.25	.23	.24	.22	.21	.19	.21	.19	.18	.16	.18	.17	.15	.13	.16	.14	.13	.11	.16	.13	.11	.08
9	.39	.37	.36	.34	.32	.30	.29	.27	.27	.26	.24	.22	.24	.22	.20	.19	.21	.19	.18	.16	.18	.17	.15	.13	.16	.15	.13	.12
10	.43	.42	.40	.39	.35	.33	.32	.31	.30	.29	.27	.26	.26	.25	.23	.22	.23	.22	.20	.19	.20	.19	.17	.16	.18	.17	.15	.14
11	.48	.46	.45	.43	.39	.38	.36	.34	.34	.32	.30	.29	.29	.28	.26	.24	.26	.24	.23	.21	.23	.21	.19	.18	.20	.19	.17	.16
12	.52	.51	.49	.48	.43	.41	.40	.38	.37	.35	.34	.32	.32	.30	.29	.27	.28	.27	.25	.24	.25	.23	.22	.20	.22	.21	.19	.18
13	---	---	.54	.52	---	---	.43	.42	---	---	.37	.35	---	---	.32	.30	---	---	.28	.26	---	---	.24	.22	---	---	.21	.20
14	---	---	.58	.57	---	---	.47	.45	---	---	.40	.38	---	---	.34	.33	---	---	.30	.29	---	---	.26	.24	---	---	.23	.22
15	---	---	---	.61	---	---	---	.59	---	---	---	.42	---	---	---	.36	---	---	---	.31	---	---	---	.27	---	---	---	.24
16	---	---	---	.66	---	---	---	.53	---	---	---	.45	---	---	---	.38	---	---	---	.34	---	---	---	.23	---	---	---	.26

Drinking Pattern. Individual drinking patterns significantly impact BAC levels. Drinking at a constant pace over time will generally result in a more predictable BAC. For example, drinking two beers per hour for five hours will create a lower BAC than guzzling a pitcher of beer one hour before a chemical test. The rapid consumption of alcohol can skyrocket BAC levels. Consequently, waiting several hours after the consumption of alcohol is better than constant drinking up to the time of driving.

In rare instances, however, binge drinking can be advantageous. For example, if a chemical test is performed immediately after the rapid consumption of alcohol, the BAC result will be relatively low because the alcohol did not have time to absorb into the bloodstream. Obviously, the amount of alcohol consumed will impact BAC levels, but do not discount the importance of monitoring individual drinking patterns.

Biological Factors. BAC levels are affected by biological influences, such as metabolism, alcohol absorption, and sleep deprivation. These biological factors are silent variables in the BAC equation, and therefore impossible to predict and equally impossible to estimate. Only experience can best answer this question. Attempt to monitor the amount of alcohol consumed and how it impacts your faculties. Although not a precise science, it offers one more safeguard before drinking and driving.

Carbonated Beverages. BAC levels are influenced by beverage carbonation, which accelerates alcohol absorption rates. In other words, a whiskey-sour mixed drink will absorb faster than vodka and orange juice. *Strategy:* Mix alcohol with water or fruit juices to stabilize BAC levels.

Drugs and Medication. Always remember the impact of mixing alcohol and drugs, whether illegal, prescription or over-the-counter. It is unlawful to operate a motor vehicle after consuming alcohol and drugs if it impairs driving abilities, and only in remote circumstances will the law create an exception to this general rule. (*See* Chapter 3). Consult a pharmacist to determine whether mixing alcohol and medications will cause driving impairment.

Proving Intoxication

Most states use objective and subjective methods of establishing intoxicated driving. Obviously, from a defense attorney's perspective, the subjective test is the easiest to refute because it deals with indicators of intoxication, not scientific evidence. Nevertheless, it is important for motorists to understand both aspects of determining intoxication.

Objective Test. The objective chemical test involves scientific and medical evidence to establish the BAC level of motorists. Scientific diagnostic equipment calculates BAC levels by monitoring body specimens of blood, breath or urine. Testing reliability depends upon various factors, but generally the breath result is considered least reliable and the blood test most reliable.

There are numerous factors that affect the reliability of chemical test results. Each test involves a series of calculations using scientific theories based upon the average person. Since the tests fail to consider other factors, the results may not accurately reflect the defendant's BAC level. (The reliability of BAC results is discussed in Chapter 7.)

Subjective Test. The subjective test utilizes sensory perceptions to identify and describe intoxicated behavior. Testimony is frequently from a police officer trained in detecting the indicators of intoxication who can verify the defendant exhibited consistent behavior. Typical subjective indicators of intoxication include bloodshot/watery eyes, smell of alcohol, unsteady balance, flushed face, slurred speech, and either despondent or excited behavior. Obviously, it is easier to refute the subjective indicators of intoxication because the defendant can present logical explanations for the alleged intoxicated behavior. (Refuting the subjective indicators of intoxication is discussed in Chapter 5.)

BAC Levels When Driving Occurred. The key to prosecuting a drunk driving case is proving the motorist's BAC level at the time of driving. For a conviction, the driver must be legally intoxicated at the time of operating a motor vehicle. Consequently, any lapse of time between driving and the chemical test can significantly affect the BAC level, as does the consumption of alcohol *after* driving. Both hinder the prosecutor's ability to obtain a drunk driving conviction.

For instance, if more than two hours lapse between driving and a chemical test, defense counsel can often show the defendant's BAC was below the legal limit at the time of driving. Since the human body continuously metabolizes alcohol, an extended delay can dramatically affect BAC results.

Similarly, the consumption of alcohol after the alleged driving will skew BAC results. In one case, the defendant was involved in an accident, walked to a tavern, and consumed alcohol before the police arrived to investigate. The chemical test indicated a BAC above the legal limit, but some of the alcohol was consumed after the accident. The distorted chemical test result made it very difficult for the prosecutor to prove the defendant was legally intoxicated when the driving occurred.

Even though the prosecutor will infer that the consumption of alcohol was a purposeful act to distort the chemical test result, the defendant can offer expert testimony to verify that many individuals resort to alcohol to calm their nerves after a harrowing experience, such as an automobile accident. Of course, defense attorneys cannot advocate the consumption of alcohol solely to avoid a drunk driving charge, but it does occur and defendants have successfully used this logical explanation to justify their behavior.

Proving Drug Use

The other means of prosecuting motorists for drunk driving is the operation of a motor vehicle while under the influence of drugs or a combination of drugs and alcohol. If a person is taking prescribed medication under the direction of a licensed physician, and the operation of a motor vehicle is not restricted, then a person may lawfully drive. However, if there is no prescription, the substance is illegal, or a physician does not authorize driving, then a motorist can be prosecuted and convicted of drunk driving. This rule also applies to over-the-counter drugs.

Legal Definition. Although there is no case law defining the parameters of what constitutes a drug, the element of proof is whether the substance impaired driving abilities to any extent. If a motorist is buzzing from a caffeine high, the state could prosecute the person for drunk driving. In one instance, a person was convicted for lawfully using insulin.

Consult with a Pharmacist. It is always best to consult with your treating physician or regular pharmacist regarding the safe operation of a vehicle or whether specific medications can be consumed with alcohol. If there are warnings against the consumption of alcohol, it is more likely that criminal charges will be brought under the drunk driving statute, even though the medication was prescribed.

Drug Tests. The NHTSA established eight field sobriety tests to determine drug usage: horizontal gaze nystagmus (HGN), pupil reaction, pupil size, standing steadiness, one-leg stand, walk-the-line, finger-to-nose, and pulse rate. Officers also consider skin marks, apathy, drowsiness, and hyperactivity. Although relatively accurate indicators of drug use, the reliability of the results is contingent upon the training and experience of the officer administering the tests.

3

Legal Defenses

Previous chapters outlined the legal requirements for convicting motorists of drunk driving and subsequent chapters will discuss ways to refute prosecutorial evidence. This chapter presents legal justifications for driving drunk and acceptable defenses that may be asserted to avoid a drunk driving conviction. By asserting these defenses, the motorist does not necessarily deny being intoxicated, but claims a valid reason for breaking the law to justify driving in such a condition.

There are five common legal excuses--necessity, entrapment, duress, mistake of fact, and lawfully prescribed medication--but other excuses may be asserted depending upon individual circumstances. Although legal defenses can be raised, few are applicable to drunk driving charges. Nevertheless, it is necessary to understand the legal rights of motorists because individual circumstances may warrant using one of these defenses in the future.

Necessity

The defense of necessity requires some urgent event that prompts a motorist to choose between the lesser of two evils, one of which is driving drunk. To qualify for this defense the driver must be in the process of avoiding imminent danger to life or property, the danger must be immediate, and the driving must occur before the danger has passed. Moreover, the driver must admit to driving drunk at the time of the incident.

For example, two men were in a bar fight, and one person was seriously injured. The defendant raised legal necessity as a defense since he was driving a friend to the hospital. Although an appropriate defense, the police stop occurred over two hours after the fight. The defendant claimed there was a flat tire, but the jury did not believe the injury was serious because an ambulance could have been called and they were only a short distance from the hospital.

Entrapment

There is relatively little case law discussing entrapment as a defense to drunk driving because it is unlikely that police officers could lure a person into drinking and then entice the drunkard into driving. Entrapment requires the police to create an environment that lures bystanders into criminal activity. In the drunk driving context, it is nearly impossible to imagine a scenario where police conduct constitutes entrapment.

Duress

Like the defense of entrapment, duress is equally rare and highly unlikely to arise in the drunk driving context. The factual circumstances would require police officers to coerce an individual, through violence or comparable threats, to drive a vehicle. For the person to leave the scene, the officer's threat must be more than a mere order or directive; it must be substantial and the actual physical violence significant.

In one of the few cases on the subject, a parking lot argument attracted the attention of two police officers. A nightstick was used on one of the subjects and the other was told to leave the scene. The officer raised the nightstick, so the subject entered his truck and accidentally backed into the police car. He was arrested for drunk driving, and the court upheld the conviction because the police conduct did not constitute duress.

Mistake of Fact

Mistake of fact arises when defendants truly believe they are not legally intoxicated. Although a rare instance, and still subject to prosecution for being impaired, this legal defense can be raised to avoid a conviction. It requires an honest and reasonable belief that the defendant was not intoxicated; if the reasonable belief was true and accurate, the resulting conduct is considered lawful and proper.

In one circumstance, the driver was arrested for drunk driving and the passenger was given a PBT. The result was below the legal limit, so the officer instructed the passenger to drive the vehicle home. The person was subsequently stopped by a different police officer and charged with drunk driving. In this instance, the defendant properly raised a valid legal defense.

Arguably, a motorist can allege a mistaken belief about the impact of a certain drug on their ability to drive. If there is evidence the motorist consumed medication, was never informed of the impairing effect on their driving ability, and there was no reason to anticipate or otherwise know the effects, the defendant can use this defense to challenge a drunk driving charge.

Medication

Operating a motor vehicle while under the influence of a drug is sufficient to establish a drunk driving charge, even if the drug is lawful, over-the-counter, or physically necessary. The only legal requirement is that the drug impairs driving abilities. However, there is an exception to the rule. If the drug was lawfully prescribed by a licensed medical practitioner, the appropriate dosage was consumed without alcohol, and the patient was not notified that driving was prohibited, then it may be lawful to operate a motor vehicle.

4

Police Stop

One of the most harrowing incidents a motorist will encounter is having their vehicle stopped by a police officer. As the swirling lights appear in the rearview mirror, most motorists experience heart palpitations, nervous energy and rampant anxiety. The fear intensifies during evening hours, especially after consuming alcohol, because the police often target drunk drivers for an "easy" conviction.

Some officers ask every driver to perform field sobriety tests. Regardless of the amount of alcohol consumed or the officer's expertise at recognizing the indicators of intoxication, from 11 p.m. until 5 a.m., every driver is ordered to exit the vehicle and perform the tests. This is an egregious abuse of police power. To require sober motorists to perform roadside field sobriety tests, in the absence of probable cause of intoxication, is humiliating and offensive to the American justice system. The purpose of this chapter is to inform every motorist of their rights during a police stop.

Vehicle Stop

Recent legal trends expand the authority of police officers at the expense of individual rights. Officers are given broad discretion to perform functions that were once forbidden, but are now deemed within the line of duty. In the future, expect fewer constitutional rights for defendants and more restricted privacy interests for motorists.

Probable Cause. A police stop occurs when an officer physically detains a motorist based upon probable cause that criminal activity has occurred. When the vehicle is moving, motorists have a reasonable expectation of privacy and officers must have probable cause to initiate a police stop. On the other hand, if a vehicle is parked outside a bank in what appears to be a stakeout, officers may detain the driver to inquire about any suspicious behavior.

To substantiate a police stop the officer must establish probable cause that a law violation occurred. Over the last quarter-century, this legal requirement has withered with each judicial precedent. In the past, motorists could expect a police stop for speeding or reckless driving, and even such innocuous infractions as a defective taillight.

At the present time, officers can stop a vehicle when no law violation has occurred. Simply weaving within the lane but never crossing the painted lines is sufficient to justify a police stop. The police can also create probable cause by running a license plate check; if the owner's description matches the driver of the vehicle, the officer will perform a license check to determine whether it is lawful for the motorist to drive. If the license is invalid, a police stop and arrest is appropriate.

Suppressing Evidence. In rare instances the defendant can suppress evidence when an officer lacks probable cause for a police stop. It is insufficient to justify a police stop based upon the mere suspicion that criminal activity is afoot; absent probable cause, any arrest or criminal charge is illegal. For instance, a sting operation to stop every vehicle leaving the parking lot of a particular tavern is illegal because it lacks probable cause.

If an officer requests field sobriety tests without probable cause of drunk driving, the test result evidence should be suppressed. According to the courts, field sobriety tests are full searches and therefore subject to constitutional protection. In fact, the tests are considered more intrusive than chemical testing because the activity is publicly displayed.

Vehicle Search

Although vehicle searches are not a serious problem during a typical police stop, the issue is important if the occupants possess illegal drugs or other contraband. In these situations, as well as others, it is vital to know your rights to recognize an unlawful police search.

Vehicle Compartments. The law empowers officers to implement vehicle searches with greater ease and less probable cause. Police can lawfully peer through windows to observe the interior of vehicles, but once inside, motorists are afforded greater constitutional protection. For instance, the trunk and glove box are given some privacy protection because they are enclosed compartments. Glove boxes are more easily inspected if the compartment is not locked; however, even a locked glove box can be searched because of its accessibility to the driver and passenger. The trunk is more private because it is not accessible to vehicle occupants, but this does not apply to hatchbacks, vans or station wagons. Despite all the privacy interests, if the vehicle is impounded, officers are usually allowed to search these areas to inventory the vehicle's contents.

Non-vehicle Containers. Vehicle occupants have an even greater privacy interest when the search involves enclosed containers within the vehicle. Passengers have the right to refuse a police officer's request to search containers that are not typically part of the vehicle. For example, purses are highly private and personal containers that are not part of a vehicle, and therefore receive the most constitutional protection.

Other common containers include coolers, lock boxes, paper bags, tackle boxes, cardboard boxes, etc. The list of potentially private containers is endless. Even after an arrest, the police do not have unlimited authority to conduct an inventory search of every compartment. They usually need a court order. Since the constitutional protection of individual compartments varies depending upon the container and the facts of each case, it is important to realize that citizens are afforded some constitutional protection.

Inventory Searches. Despite the subtle nuances of privacy interests and constitutional guarantees, most individual rights are nullified by legal technicalities. If the police are able to initiate an arrest, which is allowed for any offense--even traffic tickets--then the vehicle can be impounded and inventoried. The purpose of the inventory is to protect the vehicle owner against theft, but the result is the same--unbridled police authority. If the police discover stolen items or illegal substances during an inventory search, additional criminal charges can be filed against the vehicle owners or occupants.

Constitutional protection hinges on the level of intrusiveness. For instance, if the officer inspects every piece of paper in a wallet, it is most likely an unconstitutional infringement. Similarly, if the officer searches every compartment of a purse, a constitutional challenge may be available. Since constitutional rights are specific to a particular case, no all-inclusive rule can provide assurances so consult an attorney to discuss the ramifications of questionable police searches.

Owner Rights

The rights of parties associated with a police stop vary depending upon the circumstances of each case, knowledge of illegal activity, and the amount of control over the vehicle or its contents. In drunk driving cases, the vehicle owner's concerns often involve illegal substances or impoundment issues. In some instances, the vehicle owner is responsible for illegal contents and the actions of the driver.

Illegal Substance. When an illegal substance is found in a vehicle and the owner is not present, the vehicle occupants are often held responsible. The old adage: possession is 9/10ths of the law, is applicable to this context. Of course, this rule is not absolute and the owner could face criminal charges, especially if the illegal substance is in a locked glove box or other concealed compartment that is not accessible to the vehicle occupants.

Vehicle Impoundment. Even if the vehicle owner is not involved in a drunk driving incident, in certain instances the vehicle can be seized, impounded or sold. Typically, statutes require the owner to have knowledge of two things: 1) the driver has a prior drunk driving offense; and 2) the vehicle will be used in conjunction with the consumption of alcohol. Although "knowledge" is difficult to prove, it can be a major inconvenience to resolve this misunderstanding in court.

Strategy: Prior to the sentencing hearing, transfer the vehicle title into the name of someone having no association with the drunk driving incident, such as a friend or relative. This eliminates any seizure, impound or auction issues, and allows the owner to retain possession of the vehicle. One day after the sentencing hearing, transfer title to the original owner. In some instances the defendant cannot register a vehicle until the driver's license suspension period has expired. Under these circumstances, transfer title into the name of a third-party having no connection with the drunk driving incident.

Driver Rights

In comparison to passenger rights, drivers are held more accountable because they have control of the vehicle. When an illegal substance is discovered, the driver is first to blame. Of course, physical proximity affects the issue of possession. If the substance is located on the passenger floorboard, the driver is less likely to be charged; if the illegal substance is located *under* the passenger seat, either party could be charged. Contents located in the trunk, glove box, center console, or other hidden locales are likely to be viewed as the responsibility of the driver.

Once again, this is a generalization about police perspectives on criminal activity. The result can vary with individual officers, the appearance and demeanor of the vehicle occupants, or their criminal history. The fact that criminal charges are brought does not necessarily translate into a conviction. Often vehicle searches cause problems for prosecutors because they cannot prove actual or constructive possession of the illegal substance.

Passenger Rights

The passenger is afforded the greatest constitutional protection and police deference. Since the passenger is often a captive occupant of the vehicle and unable to control their destination, police are less likely to press criminal charges. The lack of control is a key factor when evaluating passenger rights.

5

Indicators of Intoxication

During the initial police stop, officers consider numerous factors to substantiate a drunk driving charge. Although many of the considerations are only remotely related to drunk driving, each test is characterized as strong evidence of intoxication. Since most police stops are predicated on a traffic violation, the purpose of this chapter is to illustrate the errors in equating traffic violations with allegations of drunk driving.

Another consideration is the police officer's observations after initiating contact with the defendant. During a police stop, officers observe the driver to determine whether the signs of intoxication exist. Basically, officers evaluate the motorist's physical coordination, speech pattern, appearance and behavior. This chapter is designed to offer useful information so motorists can present the best image of sobriety.

Driving Behavior

In nearly every drunk driving arrest an officer alleges that the defendant was operating a motor vehicle in a manner consistent with impairment. Although ordinary driving errors can occur without the presence of alcohol, it is important to educate the jury about this fact. When confronting the officer at trial, the goal is to minimize the negative implication of intoxication and create a positive image of sobriety.

A typical drunk driving arrest involves speeding, weaving in the lane, failure to come to a complete stop, or delayed reaction in pulling to the side of the road. In each instance, legitimate explanations can be offered to minimize the inference of intoxication.

Speeding. Speeding is a common traffic violation that most motorists encounter in their everyday driving experience, and only in rare instances is the driver intoxicated. Nevertheless, the officer will testify that speeding is a classic example of drunken behavior because alcohol impairs judgment and intoxicated drivers frequently speed. Defendants can neutralize this negative testimony by offering evidence that high-speed driving requires greater skill and coordination.

Weaving. Another common driving pattern often attributed to drunken driving is weaving within a lane. Since everyone weaves in the lane, the degree and frequency is crucial to determine the legitimacy of a police stop. Defense counsel can refute the inference of impairment by showing that all vehicles weave within their lane and that the driver never crossed the painted lines. The driver can also present other explanations for weaving: mechanical problems, road conditions, width of road, white-line-fever or black-and-white fever.

Complete Stops. Failing to make a complete stop is another driving behavior unrelated to intoxication. Police like to characterize this behavior as an indicator of intoxication but in reality it is simply inattentive driving or impatience.

Delayed Reaction. In many drunk driving arrests the officer specifically mentions that the motorist failed to immediately pull to the side of the road. The inference is that a slower reaction is the result of intoxication. On the contrary, this behavior often has a logical explanation: 1) believing the stop is intended for someone else; 2) failing to regularly check the rearview mirror; 3) searching for a better place to stop to avoid being a traffic hazard; or 4) difficulty seeing the lights during daylight hours. If the siren was activated, the driver may have been distracted, daydreaming, talking on a cellular phone, or playing the radio too loud.

Positive Perspective

At trial, it is imperative to present a positive perspective of the relevant facts. The ultimate goal is to present a logical explanation for the defendant's allegedly erratic driving behavior. Officers will skew evidence favorably for the prosecution, so defendants must also present an alternative perspective. This provides the jury with an opportunity to select the most credible explanation.

Defense attorneys should cross-examine officers about every aspect of the defendant's driving behavior--rapid acceleration or deceleration, traveling too slow, hugging the shoulder of the road, etc.--to illustrate that the defendant performed these tests without exhibiting signs of intoxication. Once a lengthy list is compiled, it minimizes the importance of the defendant's erratic driving and infers that intoxication was not involved in the driving behavior.

Furthermore, if the officer has a lengthy list of traffic violations prior to implementing a police stop, it is important to explain the lack of seriousness associated with these infractions. If the defendant is endangering lives or driving haphazardly, the officer should immediately arrest the defendant instead of following the vehicle for an extended distance to compile a lengthy list of violations.

The NHTSA conducted a study of various driving infractions that are often associated with drunk driving. (*See* Chart 4). Jurors are often shocked to discover that 40 out of 100 drivers who "appear to be drunk" to police officers, are in fact, not under the influence. Similarly, 40 out of 100 drivers who nearly strike another vehicle are legally sober.

Since officers rarely observe traffic violations in isolation, the NHTSA study also indicates the likelihood of a driver being intoxicated when multiple infractions are observed. When two or more cues are present, add 10 to the highest value among the cues observed. For example, if the subject is weaving (60), following too close (45), and driving without headlights (30), there is a 70% chance the driver has a BAC of .10 or more.

Appearance and Demeanor

It is almost universally accepted that the indicators of intoxication are fatally flawed because sober individuals can be characterized as drunk drivers. According to legislative findings, there are approximately 60 pathological conditions that exhibit symptoms of alcohol consumption, despite the lack of alcohol being present. Alcohol symptoms may be the product of illness or medication, insulin

Chart 4

Detecting Drunk Drivers at Night

Turning with wide radius	65
Straddling center or lane marker	65
Appearing to be drunk	60
Almost striking object or vehicle	60
Weaving	60
Driving on other than designated roadway	55
Swerving	55
Slow speed (more than 10 m.p.h. below limit)	50
Stopping (without cause) in traffic lane	50
Drifting	50
Following too close	45
Tires on center or lane marker	45
Braking erratically	45
Driving into opposing or crossing traffic	45
Signaling inconsistent with driving actions	40
Stopping inappropriately (other than in lane)	35
Turning abruptly or illegally	35
Accelerating or decelerating rapidly	30
Headlights off	30

Note: Shows the chances out of 100 that a driver has a BAC of .10 or higher.

overdose or deficiency, nervous system injuries, concussions, or hypoglycemia.

Nevertheless, officers are adamant that their observations conclusively prove intoxication. The following is a list of the most frequently cited activities that indicate intoxicated behavior:

1) odor of alcohol
2) fumbling with wallet
3) bloodshot, watery or glassy eyes
4) slurred or thick speech
5) flushed complexion
6) staggering and stumbling
7) clothing in disarray or poor grooming
8) rambling or despondent

To rebut this evidence, it is important to give a reasonable explanation for the "intoxicated" behavior. Since each indicator of intoxication can be refuted with legitimate sober behavior, the defendant can create reasonable doubt to gain an acquittal.

Odor of Alcohol. The smell of alcohol is often cited as a contributing factor in the officer's determination of intoxication. However, alcohol is odorless, so the officer is actually testifying about the flavoring inherent in most beverages. Ironically, beer and wine have significantly stronger odors than hard liquor so a person can drink far less beer and wine yet smell worse than someone consuming larger quantities of hard liquor. The odor has no correlation to the amount of alcohol consumed, so an officer cannot testify about how much alcohol was ingested or when it was consumed.

There are other sources that contribute to the smell of alcohol. Products that remain in the throat for extended periods of time are contributing factors, such as mouthwash, cough syrup, or deodorizing throat spray. Syrupy alcoholic beverages--Kahlúa or other liqueurs-- tend to remain in the throat for longer periods of time so the smell will be stronger. Moreover, certain illnesses can create a breath comparable to the "odor of alcohol" and belching causes gaseous odors to remain in the throat for approximately ten minutes.

Strategy: Most chemical breath tests prohibit operation within ten minutes of belching, so some defendants have delayed the test by swallowing air to facilitate a belch. This is especially useful to possibly avoid the driver's license suspension for a test refusal. If a test is given, the result is inadmissible; if no test is given, the defendant was cooperative, but has a legitimate excuse--uncontrollable belching.

Alcohol generally requires one hour to have the maximum effect on the body. If the officer claims that a strong smell of alcohol indicates recent consumption, then defense counsel can argue that the defendant was not legally drunk at the time of driving because the alcohol did not have time to absorb into the bloodstream.

It is important to note that the smell of alcoholic beverages usually triggers police suspicion of a possible drunk driver. Thereafter, the officer will search for additional evidence of intoxication to substantiate a criminal charge. *Strategy:* To protect individual privacy from overly intrusive officers, motorists must learn to conceal their breath. There are numerous products on the market designed for breath concealment, so make an informed selection. Nu-Breath® works for some, while others prefer red-hot cinnamon, pungent candy or gum. Using the appropriate product before initiating contact with an officer will help conceal offensive breath odors.

Bloodshot Eyes. Another common indicator of intoxication is bloodshot, watery eyes. There are numerous explanations for red eyes: 1) fatigue or insomnia; 2) exposure to dusty, hot or windy conditions; 3) normal eye condition; 4) eye irritation from a foreign object; 5) old or dirty contact lenses; 6) air pollution; 7) allergies; 8) extensive reading; or 9) significant eye strain.

Slurred Speech. One frequently cited indicator of intoxication is thick or slurred speech. Of course, only in rare instances would the officer have prior contact with the motorist, so it is nearly impossible to know the defendant's regular speech pattern. To rebut this evidence, the defendant should testify to illustrate a consistent speech pattern. The other option is testimony from a witness who observed the defendant moments before or after the arrest, or someone familiar with the defendant's normal speech pattern.

Be prepared to present other explanations for slurred speech, such as medical or dental problems. Do not forget that the speech impediment could be the product of gum or candy in the defendant's mouth while conversing with the officer. Your attorney should also mention that the officer was able to understand the defendant's response to various questions, despite the allegation of slurred speech.

Flushed Face. A flushed face is often cited as evidence of intoxication, though it is not uncommon for people to have a crimson complexion. If the officer had no prior contact with the defendant, then evidence of the defendant's natural appearance is the best explanation. Likewise, older persons are more apt to have reddish complexioned skin, which is a natural process of aging, and not necessarily evidence of intoxication. Many motorists have a flushed face during a police stop due to nervousness, fear, embarrassment or anger. Medication and excessive makeup are contributing factors, as well as a wind-chapped face from cold weather.

Coordination. Testimony that a driver was fumbling with their wallet is supposed to indicate a lack of coordination caused by the excessive consumption of alcohol. To defend against this allegation of intoxicated behavior, the motorist must present a reasonable explanation, such as nervousness during the police stop or a prior hand injury.

Moreover, when the driver is accused of staggering, stumbling or needing a brace to stand erect, it is important to analyze the circumstances surrounding the alleged drunken behavior. If this behavior occurred only once, then it could be the result of poor blood circulation, arthritis, sitting in a cramped position for an extended period of time, or quivering muscles from nervousness or inclement weather. Typically, the initial exit from a vehicle results in imbalance and incoordination.

If there are multiple instances of imbalance, the behavior must be analyzed in the context of other field sobriety tests. If physical performance field sobriety tests were used, the officer should have mentioned repeated acts of staggering, stumbling, or using a brace. Other considerations: 1) medical explanations, e.g., back, leg or foot injury, or inner ear disorder; 2) high heel shoes or defective soles; or 3) irregular or uneven road surface.

Poor Grooming. Clothes in disarray or unkempt grooming is often cited as an indicator of intoxication. It is important to present reasonable explanations for an irregular appearance. Obviously, after spending a full day in the same clothes many explanations are available--natural wrinkling; napping in the same set of clothes; wearing work clothes in an inherently dirty environment; or simply for comfort.

Similarly, unkempt hair is supposed to correlate with drunkenness, but this can result from wind or not possessing a comb. Scruffy facial hair can be caused by rapid hair growth or personal preference. Dark-haired persons often have a noticeable 5-o'clock shadow, and some people have sensitive skin that inhibits daily shaving.

Rambling or Despondency. This is a double-edged sword. A talkative disposition indicates impairment because of visibly excited emotions; however, despondency is evidence of intoxication because alcohol is a depressant. Thus, it is ludicrous to use either factor as evidence of intoxication.

6

Field Sobriety Tests

If you encounter a police officer who requires every driver to perform field sobriety tests, it is imperative to know your legal rights. The moment an officer institutes a police stop, motorists have some constitutional protection. Although officers have a certain level of discretion to control the vehicle's occupants, there is a gray area between lawful and unconstitutional police action. Since legal rights are defined by courts using specific factual circumstances, the following illustrations offer guidance to motorists, not definitive answers to particular scenarios.

Police Stop

A typical police stop commences with a brief discussion regarding the purpose of the stop. This allows the officer to approach the vehicle and observe the driver, passenger(s), or vehicle contents. In a drunk driving stop, the officer uses this opportunity to smell the interior of the vehicle and monitor the driver's physical appearance and behavior. At this moment the officer will ask whether the driver had anything to drink. Naturally, the answer is a double-edged sword.

If the driver denies consuming alcohol, the officer will undoubtedly order the driver to exit the vehicle and perform field sobriety tests. The officer will also use the potentially incriminating answer at trial. On the other hand, by admitting to the consumption of alcohol, the officer will still order the driver to perform field sobriety tests and use the incriminating response at trial.

Although there are exceptions to the rule, most officers attempt to build the strongest possible case to win a conviction. Unfortunately, most motorists believe they can talk their way out of a drunk driving charge. This is far from the truth. The police have a legal duty to arrest law violators and testify against them, so the more you say, the easier it is to convict. Before speaking, consider all your legal rights so you can make a rational decision.

Field Sobriety Tests - Generally

Every law enforcement officer is trained to administer three nationally standardized field sobriety tests--horizontal gaze nystagmus (HGN), walk-the-line, and one-leg stand. The tests are frequently heralded by prosecutors and law enforcement advocates as ideal for determining intoxication because they involve divided-attention activities (one-leg lift and walk-the-line) or involuntary responses (HGN). Standardized field sobriety tests are supposed to make convictions easier by providing consistent evidence of driver intoxication.

The one-leg lift has the subject counting to 30 while holding one leg in the air. The walk-the-line test involves counting nine steps while walking heel-to-toe, then turning around and repeating the same activity. Each test divides attention between mental tasks (counting) and physical acts (lifting one leg or walking heel-to-toe). In theory, alcohol inhibits the ability to adequately perform these activities, so a test failure indicates intoxication.

The HGN is not a divided-attention test; instead it measures a physically involuntary response of the eye. Prosecutors praise the test as offering solid proof of intoxication because the test cannot be practiced and therefore the results cannot be distorted.

Divided-Attention Tests

Despite the praise given to divided-attention field sobriety tests, advocates fail to mention the limitations and unreliability of the tests. For instance, driving a vehicle is a divided-attention task. Motorists are required to process numerous mental impressions while physically operating the accelerator, brake or clutch. In other words, any motorist stopped for a faulty taillight, and not erratic driving, has properly performed a divided-attention activity that is more rigorous than the standardized field sobriety tests.

Obeying Traffic Laws. The mere failure to obey a traffic law is not evidence of intoxication. Thousands of motorists are stopped every day for speeding, failing to come to a complete stop, running a red light, weaving in their lane, or crossing the centerline. The list is endless. But in each instance, very few motorists are actually drunk, despite failing to properly perform a divided-attention activity. (*See* Chart 4).

Subjective Tests. Another significant error of the field sobriety tests is a lack of objectivity. Test results are based upon the officer's biased observations. The mere fact that an officer is having a motorist perform field sobriety tests is an indication that the officer believes the driver is impaired. This presumption of intoxication will consciously or subconsciously distort the officer's perception of the motorist's test performance. Soon, normal behavior is documented as evidence of intoxication. For example, a motorist was asked to perform a non-standardized field sobriety test, counting backwards from 110 to 83. He recited the numbers perfectly and kept counting backwards to prove he was fully cognizant; however, the officer interpreted this noncompliance as evidence of intoxication because the motorist did not follow directions by stopping at 83.

Strategy: Humans are notorious for showing off. In the context of police stops and field sobriety tests, motorists must learn to curb their insatiable appetite for attention and praise. In the walk-the-line test, walking more than nine steps is a test failure for not following directions, rather than an impressive display of sobriety. Similarly, in the one-leg lift, maintaining a raised leg for more than 30 seconds is also a test failure for not obeying instructions.

Reliability and Accuracy. Despite prosecutors heralding divided-attention tests as precise indicators of intoxication, each nationally standardized test is unreliable and inaccurate. The one-leg stand and walk-the-line tests are 65% and 68% accurate, respectively. Even the HGN has a reliability rate of only 77%. The one redeeming quality of these tests is the combined accuracy. According to one study, the triumvirate is 83.4% accurate to predict intoxication above the legal limit. Of course, the actual level of impairment remains questionable.

Laboratory Conditions. Field sobriety tests also lack credibility because the accuracy percentages are based upon ideal laboratory testing conditions. The one-leg lift was originally performed on a perfectly level and smooth surface. During a typical traffic stop, the test is performed on an irregular or rough surface that can affect balance based upon the manner in which the shoe meets the pavement.

There are other precautions that skew results for the one-leg lift. Due to balance problems, the test should not be given to individuals more than 50 pounds overweight or above 60 years of age, and the test is not effective if the person has physical problems that affect balance, such as leg and back injuries or inner ear disorders. Moreover, the lighting must be adequate because the test cannot be performed in darkness.

The walk-the-line test has similar problems. Ideal testing conditions offer sufficient lighting and straight lines to guide walking. On the scene of a police stop, the irregular or rough surface can cause unsteady balance. Furthermore, there is seldom a straight line to follow--usually a crack in the ground, edge of the pavement, or painted line on the road. Each example constitutes irregular lines, so the motorist is more likely to fail.

In addition, the walk-the-line test can produce skewed results. Due to balance problems, the test should not be given to individuals more than 50 pounds overweight or above 60 years of age, and persons with only one functional eye may have difficulty because of depth perception problems. *Strategy:* This test is easier to perform if you are not looking at your feet and keep a slight distance between heel and toe. If the officer does not instruct you to watch your feet, be sure to gaze at the horizon.

Improper Instructions. The divided-attention field sobriety tests can be challenged when the officer fails to notify the motorist of behavior that constitutes a test failure. Motorists are often fully informed on how to perform the test, but rarely does the officer reveal behavior that is considered a test failure. For example, in the walk-the-line test, it is a failure to walk too many steps, raise arms, sway the body, turn with the wrong foot, look up, miss the heel to toe, etc. When a person exhibits this behavior at any time while performing the test, it is a negative mark. The cumulative number of improperly performed aspects of the test is supposed to indicate increased alcohol impairment.

Since the motorist is rarely informed about activity that constitutes a failure, exposing the test administration bias can effectively reduce the officer's credibility. It is important to attack every aspect of the divided-attention tests because the jury is less likely to believe the officer's conclusions when the results are based upon inadequate testing procedures.

Involuntary Field Sobriety Tests

The Horizontal Gaze Nystagmus (HGN) is the third nationally standardized field sobriety test. In this test, the officer monitors the defendant's eyes, which are following a moving object, usually the tip of a pen. The pen is approximately six inches from the defendant's nose, and slowly moved toward each shoulder and then toward the forehead and chest. If the eye begins jerking, as opposed to a smooth pursuit, before the pen reaches a 45-degree angle, this represents alcohol impairment.

Accuracy. Of all the field sobriety tests, the HGN is most accurate, though it is only 77% reliable. In other words, 23 out of 100 individuals would fail the test despite being sober.

Laboratory Conditions. Although the HGN measures an involuntary physical response, it still has serious flaws. The test's accuracy is a product of ideal laboratory conditions--adequate lighting and precise measuring devices. In most drunk driving arrests, the test is performed on a dark street with officers using streetlights, headlights or a flashlight for illumination, and no instruments are available to measure a 45-degree angle. It is extremely difficult to monitor a slight jerking of the eye, and the test result is wholly unreliable at a 55-degree angle.

Chemicals and Drugs. There are other flaws with the HGN test result. Chemicals, drugs, and numerous substances can cause nystagmus (jerking of the eyes) without the presence of alcohol. For example, the ingestion of barbiturates, antihistamines, phencyclidine, depressants and anticonvulsants can cause nystagmus. Other influential substances include caffeine, nicotine or aspirin. Even atmospheric pressure influences nystagmus.

Physiological Problems. Health and biological ailments can cause nystagmus, such as a brain hemorrhage, inner ear disorder, certain congenital eye problems, measles, vertigo, influenza, streptococcus infections, epilepsy, syphilis, muscular dystrophy, motion sickness, sunstroke, hypertension, hypotension, Korsakoff's syndrome, arteriosclerosis, and psychogenetic disorders. This list is not exhaustive, so consult a physician.

Eye-related Flaws. Tired drivers can exhibit nystagmus due to prolonged use of the eyes, insufficient lighting, or strained positions. Moreover, test results can be distorted by failing to remove all corrective lenses--hard or soft contact lenses and glasses--prior to testing.

Pupil Reaction Test. Less common, though similar to the HGN, is the pupil reaction test. This measures the rate at which the pupil contracts when exposed to light--a slower contraction indicates greater alcohol impairment. Often officers will shine a flashlight in the defendant's eyes to observe pupil contraction. The test is flawed because it lacks scientific objectivity. Most officers lack training in ophthalmology, and have no knowledge of other possible causes of slow pupil reaction. For instance, over-the-counter drugs, such as allergy and sinus medications, can cause dilated pupils, even in the absence of alcohol consumption.

Non-standardized Field Sobriety Tests

Besides the NHTSA sponsored tests, other physical and verbal field sobriety tests are used to measure intoxication. Physical performance tests measure balance, while verbal tests measure mental acuity. Although officers typically administer the NHTSA field sobriety tests, sometimes nontraditional tests are used to supplement the standardized tests.

Physical Tests. There are several physical performance field sobriety tests that measure coordination. For example, standing at attention for 30 seconds to monitor body sway. This test is unreliable because studies show that drinking does not significantly affect body sway until nearly three hours after the cessation of drinking.

Another example is picking up coins from the ground. This measures eye-hand coordination and balance. Other tests can include rapidly touching the thumb to the tip of each finger on the same hand, or patting the palm of one hand with the palm and back of the other.

Hand Writing. One type of non-standardized physical field sobriety test is writing the alphabet. In theory, intoxication will cause careless penmanship. Of course, this is also the result of speed, nervousness or the type of writing utensil. An effective trial technique is comparing the defendant's signature on the night of the arrest with other signatures, such as a driver's license, booking slip, bail receipt or citation. If there is little variation, the evidence of intoxication is diminished.

A more risky technique is finding discrepancies in the officer's signature. The defense attorney should compare the handwriting on the night of the arrest with police reports in other cases. Since the officer was sober when signing these documents, any signature variation is excellent evidence to prove the test is flawed.

Verbal Tests. There are several verbal field sobriety tests that can be administered. The most common is reciting the alphabet without singing the song; or conversely, reciting the alphabet backwards. Another verbal test is counting backwards between two designated numbers. In some circumstances, test failures are the result of mental deficiencies or inadequate education, and in other instances the defendant attempts to illustrate sobriety by disobeying the officer's specific instructions.

Refusing Field Sobriety Tests

Few motorists realize that they have the right to refuse an officer's request for field sobriety tests (FSTs). There is no legal requirement that a driver must perform FSTs before or after an arrest. An officer can only request, not compel, a motorist to perform the tests. The critical issue is whether the refusal to perform FSTs is admissible as evidence of intoxication. The legal argument is threefold, and only one is necessary to justify a refusal to perform field sobriety tests:

1) There is no statutory authority that a motorist is required to perform the tests;
2) The officer did not inform the defendant that a refusal to perform the tests would be used as evidence in court (this may not be applicable in some cases); and
3) The evidence does not prove intoxication.

Be sure to have your attorney file a motion to suppress this evidence so the issue will be preserved for a possible appeal.

Factors Influencing Test Results

Since field sobriety tests are highly subjective, it is important for motorists to realize that many factors can affect an individual's performance, such as emotional or physical conditions, rigorous testing conditions, officer bias, or the inherent difficulty to the average person.

Physical Tests. On the physical field sobriety tests, numerous factors can cause imbalance: 1) weather conditions--wind, extreme temperatures or a slippery surface; 2) defendant's shoes, especially the height and shape, or material of the sole; 3) old age, arthritis, physical injuries or defects; 4) illness, common cold, allergies, sinus or ear infection; and 5) emotional conditions, such as nervousness, anger, or other factors that inhibit concentration.

Caffeine. Interestingly enough, caffeine has an adverse effect on test results. The combination of alcohol and caffeine has a greater impact on muscular coordination and accurate timing. Even minor amounts of alcohol combined with caffeine can cause a defendant to fail the field sobriety tests.

Biological Clock. Another contributing factor is the circadian rhythm, which involves the 24-hour biological clock in humans. Persons are more likely to perform poorly on field sobriety tests at midnight or early morning hours. Similarly, a person experiencing jet lag will perform the tests less adeptly than usual.

Suppressing Police Evidence

In drunk driving cases, the Miranda advisement is critical because incriminating evidence may be excluded at trial. The advisement is a legal duty imposed upon officers at the time of arrest to inform defendants of their right to be silent, have an attorney present, and avoid self-incrimination. The advisement is only important if the motorist provides incriminating statements to the officers after the arrest. *Strategy:* When performing field sobriety tests, never indicate that you are unable to perform these tests sober. This is an admission of impairment, and can be used as evidence at trial.

Scope of Police Authority. Officers are allowed to ask questions as part of their investigation to gather physical evidence, but cannot acquire testimonial evidence. In other words, an officer can ask questions to discern slurred speech, but cannot ask questions where the content of the answer indicates evidence of intoxication.

For example, an officer can ask questions about a person's likes and dislikes, but not the time of day, current location, day of the week, etc. The latter is testimonial evidence and subject to suppression. Even verbal field sobriety tests, such as reciting the alphabet, may require a Miranda advisement because they are testimonial in nature.

In many drunk driving cases the officer fails to advise motorists of their rights. This can be an important suppression issue if there is potentially damaging evidence, namely intake questionnaires that detail the defendant's escapades prior to the arrest.

Suppressing Field Sobriety Tests. Field sobriety tests should be attacked through a motion to suppress. Defendants are advised to discuss these issues with an attorney.

According to prosecutors, standardized field sobriety tests are based upon recognized scientific principles, i.e., if properly administered there is a direct correlation between performance and alcohol impairment. The prosecution should be required to fulfill the legal requirements that are necessary to prove the tests are scientific evidence. Naturally, this is impossible because the tests lack foundational requirements for admissibility as scientific evidence and are not widely accepted within the scientific community.

Regarding the HGN, your attorney should argue that the foundational requirements were not legally satisfied for the test to be used as scientific evidence. Defense counsel should also allege that the officer is not qualified as a medical expert to testify about BAC levels. Lastly, since the HGN is intended to gauge BAC levels, it is possible to claim that the test does not meet state testing requirements for maintenance, calibration, licensing, etc.

Finally, the refusal to provide a field sobriety test should be suppressed and held inadmissible at trial because it violates the fifth amendment right against self-incrimination. The sole purpose of FST evidence is to infer guilt, so requesting a motorist to perform the test is equivalent to having them provide incriminating testimony. Thus, this evidence is irrelevant to the trial and should be excluded.

Drugs

NHTSA established several field sobriety tests to determine drug use. Eight tests were developed--one-leg stand, finger-to-nose, walk-the-line, standing steadiness, HGN, pupil reaction, pupil size, and pulse rate. Officers also consider skin marks, apathy, drowsiness, and hyperactivity. Although the tests are considered good indicators of drug use, their reliability depends on the training and experience of the officer.

Preliminary Breath Test (PBT)

The preliminary breath test (PBT) is offered at the scene of a police stop to determine motorist intoxication. The PBT is part of the implied consent law, and in a few states refusing to take the test can result in a lengthier driver's license suspension. Although the PBT result is not admissible in a criminal proceeding, it is usually admissible in a driver's license suspension hearing. Since the PBT is not accurate or widely accepted as reliable scientific evidence, it cannot be used to prove criminal guilt beyond a reasonable doubt; however it can be used to prove civil culpability by a preponderance of the evidence (more likely than not) in a driver's license suspension hearing.

PBT reliability is significantly influenced by external factors unrelated to alcohol consumption. Depending upon the PBT model used, the result can be skewed and inflated by non-ethanol components. The fuel cell PBT is distorted by the presence of acetaldehyde, methanol, isopropanol and n-propranolol. The gas sensor PBT has inflated results with the previously mentioned chemicals, as well as acetic acid, paraldehyde, and ethylene glycol. In most studies performed, the PBT was found to be 60-80% accurate.

Impact on Legal Defense

Contrary to common belief, drunk driving defendants have several options to rebut the prosecution's evidence of intoxication. Not only are the tests unreliable and inaccurate, but they are also subject to multiple interpretations. By attacking the methodology and subjective nature of field sobriety tests, defendants can present a strong case. Moreover, officers must use appropriate measuring devices, as well as fully explain behavior that constitutes a test failure. Defense counsel should always attempt to suppress the officer's testimony regarding field sobriety test results for improper instructions. The illustrations set forth in this section are some of the legal arguments that defense counsel should use to protect the rights of their clients.

7

Chemical Testing

Chemical testing made it easier for prosecutors to obtain drunk driving convictions, so state legislatures began enacting implied consent statutes to facilitate this goal. Motorists were then forced to choose between statutory compliance or constitutional defiance when consenting to a chemical test. Although touted as conclusive proof of intoxication, the three primary chemical tests (blood, breath and urine) produce distorted results and have numerous flaws. Since most officers require a breath test, many states give defendants the right to an independent chemical test by a qualified person of their choice. This chapter provides useful information on how to control BAC levels, recognize factors that distort test results, and decide whether it is best to refuse or consent to a chemical test.

Implied Consent Statutes

Every state has an implied consent statute that obligates motorists to provide a chemical specimen if the officer has probable cause to believe the motorist is driving drunk. This obligation is directly linked to driving privileges. By operating a vehicle in the state, each motorist thereby consents to this legal requirement. If a motorist refuses the test, the law imposes more stringent driver's license sanctions.

Exceptions to Implied Consent Law

The requirement that all motorists provide a chemical specimen pursuant to an implied consent statute usually applies to scientifically recognized tests (blood, breath and urine). Most states do not require motorists to submit to a PBT, which is often administered at the scene of a drunk driving arrest. Although chemical testing is mandatory, there are exceptions to this general rule of law.

Implied Consent Advisory. The implied consent statute obligates every motorist to provide a chemical specimen to measure their BAC level. The most common exception to the statutory requirement involves the police officer's legal obligation to inform each motorist of their rights. Most statutes require officers to advise defendants of their legal rights and the ramifications of taking or refusing a chemical test.

An inadequate advisory is grounds to suppress evidence of a chemical test refusal, provided it would have been admissible in court. The suppression of evidence can occur if the officer misleads the defendant about their rights, distorts the consequences of a chemical test refusal, or coerces them into compliance with threats or promises. The officer's exact words are crucial, so listen carefully to the terms used, e.g., *may* versus *shall*, or *could* versus *would*. The officer's level of clarity is significant in the judge's decision to suppress the evidence.

Miranda Rights. Another exception is the confusion over conflicting legal rights associated with Miranda rights and the implied consent statute. The Miranda advisement notifies defendants of their constitutional rights, most notably, the right to an attorney and the right against self-incrimination; on the other hand, the implied consent statute constitutes a waive of these rights. For example, few motorists know there is no constitutional right to have an attorney present when a breath test is administered. Thus, defense counsel should argue that the officer has a legal obligation to inform the motorist about this limited right.

Honest Mistake. The implied consent statute was not meant to punish citizens for their honest confusion about the law. Nevertheless, there is an obvious contradiction in the legal rights and responsibilities of motorists. Defense counsel should assert that no reasonable person could make a rational decision regarding a test refusal. A chemical test refusal could be the product of confusion about two conflicting legal rights--Miranda advisement versus implied consent statute. The former is a constitutional protection against self-incrimination, while the latter is a statutory waiver of the right against self-incrimination. The legal contradiction between constitutional rights and the implied consent statute makes it impossible for motorists to protect their self-interest. An honest misunderstanding regarding these conflicting legal requirements may win a suppression hearing to exclude evidence of a chemical test refusal.

Changing Refusal to Consent. A final exception is the defendant's prerogative to consent to a chemical test after previously refusing the test. Although some states allow the defendant to contact an attorney before consenting to a chemical test, there is no constitutional guarantee to have counsel *present*. If the defendant is denied either option, defense counsel should argue for the legal right to consent to a chemical test or consult an attorney before making this decision.

Invalid Test Refusal

Although there are circumstances when a motorist is not legally obligated to submit to a chemical test, most situations are deemed a test refusal. For instance, it is a refusal if the motorist fails to provide a sufficient breath sample or requests an alternate test other than the test selected by the officer. Motorists are required to perform the chemical test chosen by the officer, and only upon successful completion of a valid result is an independent chemical test an available option.

Valid Test Refusal

In most instances, if a police officer asks for a chemical specimen, the motorist is obligated to comply or suffer the consequences of a test refusal. Despite this general rule, there are a few legal exceptions where a defendant is allowed to refuse a chemical test.

Request Credentials. It is not a chemical test refusal for the motorist to request documentation of the blood technician's credentials. With the advent of AIDS, courts are likely to side with the motorist's health and safety concerns. If a legitimate concern is presented, the court is less likely to allow evidence of a test refusal.

Waiver Form. It is not a test refusal when the motorist protests signing a hospital waiver of liability form. If the hospital is requiring the motorist to waive all legal rights and claims for its negligence, then the motorist has a valid reason to refuse the test. Under these circumstances, a court is likely to find that the preservation of legal rights and future malpractice claims is sufficiently important to justify a chemical test refusal.

Refuse Second Test. If the motorist submits to a chemical test, then it is not a test refusal to deny the officer's request for an additional test. One chemical test is sufficient for consent. However, the administered test must provide a valid result. The motorist is not excused for attempting, but failing to satisfactorily complete, the chemical test selected by the officer.

There is an exception to the rule of one test equals compliance. If the officer suspects the motorist is under the influence of drugs or some other impairing substance, then a second test can be required to comply with the implied consent statute.

Physical Inability. Physical inability is a legitimate excuse to avoid compliance with a chemical test. Exceptions have been made when an accident victim suffers a concussion, serious injury or shock, or the driver has emphysema or another breathing disorder that prohibits deep breaths. However, at the time a chemical test is offered, the driver has a duty to disclose the infirmity so the officer can select an alternate test.

Breath Test - Distorted Results

The chemical breath test is the most predominate form of scientific testing utilized by law enforcement agencies to determine alcohol impairment. It is the cheapest, fastest, and most efficient means of processing drunk drivers. Unfortunately, it is also one of the least reliable forms of chemical testing.

Breath Compounds. Although more accurate than a PBT, the chemical breath test is also susceptible to error. Infrared breath analyzing instruments are programmed to measure ethyl alcohol, but methyl is also detected as ethanol. Inevitably, many common compounds found in human breath are often misread as ethanol. There are approximately 100 compounds within the breath at any given time, and 70-80% of these compounds have methyl within its molecular structure. When these compounds are mistaken as ethyl alcohol, the chemical breath test produces a higher BAC level than actually exists. A greater number of methyl compounds in the breath will result in a higher cumulative BAC reading. (Consult with an attorney specializing in drunk driving defense for a list of compounds in human breath.)

Exposure to Chemicals. Some studies indicate that chemical breath test results are influenced by environmental exposure to certain chemicals, such as contact cement, oil-based paints, paint removers, glues and adhesives, cleaning fluids, varnish and lacquers. Gasoline, although containing no alcohol, provides astronomically high BAC levels hours after ingestion. This can result from the accidental swallowing of gas during siphoning; despite being completely sober, the chemical breath test will indicate substantial alcohol impairment.

False Assumptions. Few people realize that chemical test results assume the defendant's BAC is at the peak level of absorption when the sample is drawn. However, since it takes one to three hours to distribute alcohol throughout the body, there is a significant discrepancy in BAC levels at various body locations. (*See* Chart 5).

For instance, venous blood more accurately indicates BAC levels within brain tissue, and is therefore a better indicator of impairment. Unfortunately, during peak absorption, the BAC level within arterial blood is higher than venous blood. Since arterial blood travels to the lungs, a chemical breath test will have a disproportionately higher BAC level. According to drunk driving laws, BAC levels are supposed to measure alcohol impairment of the brain, but current testing devices often skew BAC results and cause unjustified convictions.

Undigested Alcohol. Undigested alcohol in the mouth can dramatically distort BAC levels because the chemical breath test result measures alcohol in the lungs *and* mouth. *Strategy:* Cleanse the palate after consuming alcohol, and keep a non-alcoholic, non-carbonated beverage (juice or water) in the vehicle for the drive home. Cold water reduces alcohol vapor more than warm water, so drink refrigerated beverages. If stopped by the police, this can be an effective precaution to avoid a distorted test result.

Chart 5

Alcohol Distribution at Equilibrium

Tissue or Fluid	Distribution Ratio
Whole Blood	1.00
Blood Plasma	1.15
Brain	0.85
Liver	0.90
Skeletal Muscle	0.85
Saliva	1.10
Urine	1.35
Alveolar Breath	0.00048 (i.e., 1:2100)

Note: Illustrates the average alcohol distribution ratios of various body tissues and fluids at equilibrium.

Products Containing Alcohol. Breath fresheners and mouthwash often contain alcohol, so ingestion at the time of a police stop can significantly distort chemical breath test results. However, BAC levels return to normal approximately 10-20 minutes after ingesting these products. *Strategy:* Stock the vehicle with breath fresheners and strong candy, not necessarily to refute chemical breath test results, but to mask the odor of alcohol and minimize the chance of a drunk driving arrest.

Most cough syrup products contain alcohol, so ingestion at the time of a police stop can significantly distort PBT and chemical breath test results. The alcohol content of these products do not dissipate from the system like breath fresheners and mouthwash, so upon ingestion it becomes part of the bloodstream and impacts the BAC level. *Strategy:* Some motorists keep cough syrup in their vehicle and have been known to consume (or pretend to consume) the product during a police stop and later claim they had a cold and did not know the product contained alcohol. If the chemical test result includes alcohol that was consumed *after* the police stop, a guilty verdict is unlikely because the higher BAC result does not indicate the actual BAC level at the time of driving. (*See* Chart 6).

Chart 6

Alcohol Content of Cough and Breath Products

Product	% of Alcohol
Cough/cold remedies	
Contact Nightime	25
Nyquil	25
Comtrex liquid	20
Vicks Formula 44M	20
Vicks Formula 44	10
Tylenol Multi-Symptom	7.0
Triaminic Expectorant	5.0
Robitussin	3.5
Dimetapp D.M.	2.3
Mouthwash	
Astring-O-Sol	76
Listerine	27
Scope (original mint)	19
Close-Up	14.5
Signal	14.5
Cepacol (regular)	14
Plax	7.5
Listermint	6.5
Throat spray	
N'ICE (mint)	26
Chloraseptic (original mint)	19
Sucrets (cherry)	12

Chemical Testing - Inherent Errors

Since the chemical breath test is almost universally used by law enforcement officers, the following discussion concentrates on this test. It is only in limited circumstances that a blood test is administered, and even less frequently that a urine test is offered. Each test is subject to attack, so always consult an attorney about the complex medical evidence that is used to rebut these test results.

Whether submitting to a blood, breath or urine test, the ultimate goal is to determine BAC levels in the body. According to the law in most states, any chemical test administered two to four hours after the alleged driving is presumed to be the BAC level at the time of driving.

This presumption allows the defendant to present evidence that refutes the test result, such as recalculating the BAC level by factoring absorption and metabolic rates and numerous other factors that distort chemical test results.

Alcohol Absorption. Since alcohol continues to absorb into the bloodstream for approximately 50 minutes after the cessation of drinking, many chemical test results indicate a higher BAC level than at the time of driving. Most defendants are stopped within 15 minutes of their last consumption of alcohol, and are administered chemical tests approximately 45 minutes after the initial police stop. Naturally, the test result will be higher and the defendant could be wrongfully charged with drunk driving. Thus, it is possible to argue that the chemical test result is inaccurate because it inflates the actual BAC level at the time of driving.

Strategy: Avoid consuming alcohol for a period of time prior to driving or document the amount of alcohol consumed within one hour of driving. If a person drinks a beer and a shot for the road, this can significantly enhance the BAC result an hour later. Since breath tests are especially susceptible to erroneous BAC results, demand a blood test if you desire the most accurate indicator.

Rate of Alcohol Absorption. Alcohol absorption rates increase with cold temperatures, stress, emotional disturbances, exercise, pain or trauma. In other words, exposure to coldness during field sobriety tests can distort chemical test results; similarly, stress, fear or emotional disturbances associated with an arrest can distort test results beyond the actual BAC level at the time of driving.

In addition, the rate of alcohol absorption within the body varies considerably. The goal of drunk driving laws is to measure brain impairment caused by alcohol consumption, but certain tissues, organs and muscles absorb alcohol at different rates. (*See* Chart 5). Since the BAC level in the lungs and veins may be higher than the BAC level in the brain, distorted chemical test results could cause a wrongful drunk driving conviction.

Rate of Alcohol Metabolism. The rate at which the body metabolizes alcohol is critical to establishing BAC levels. Each individual has a different physiological composition, so the body can metabolize alcohol either slowly or rapidly. Drunk driving laws assume a fixed rate of alcohol dissipation. Therefore, a person who slowly metabolizes alcohol may have a considerably higher BAC level because the alcohol remains in the bloodstream for a longer period of time. In other words, this person could consume the same amount of alcohol as the average person, but the BAC level would be significantly higher. Since individual metabolic rates are unknown variables in alcohol dissipation, use caution when estimating BAC levels based on body weight and alcohol consumption. (*See* Charts 2 and 3).

Average Person. Chemical testing utilizes a scientific theory premised upon measuring BAC levels of the average person. The law does not accommodate for the significant range of BAC results for each individual. For the average person, chemical breath tests assume a 1:2100 ratio of alcohol in exhaled breath to alcohol in blood, when it can range from 1:1300 to 1:3000. Urine tests assume 1.3 parts of alcohol in urine is equivalent to 1 part of alcohol in blood. Although these medical ratios may not mean anything to most motorists, it is important to alert your attorney about the inherent errors in each chemical testing device.

Individual Tolerance. Individual tolerance can result in higher BAC levels with little or no physical or mental impairment. Some people, usually heavy substance abusers, can reach near-toxic BAC levels, but may not experience many of the ill effects associated with excessive alcohol consumption.

Blood. Similar to undigested alcohol, the presence of blood in the mouth can distort breath test results. A cut lip, recent dental surgery, or mouth injuries from a brawl can increase BAC levels because the chemical breath test will measure alcohol in the lungs *and* mouth. Another factor to consider, and worthy of investigation, is the composition of the defendant's blood. A blood test result can be distorted by measuring alcohol in plasma that has a high hematocrit.

Belching/Hiccups. Belching or hiccups can distort chemical breath test results. The test must be administered at least 10-15 minutes *after* belching, hiccups, regurgitation or vomiting. Thus, the officer must have the defendant under constant observation to ensure these factors do not distort the test result. If these conditions have not been satisfied, the defendant can argue to suppress the breath test result.

Products Containing Alcohol.   As previously mentioned, breath fresheners, mouthwash and cough syrup often contain alcohol, so ingestion at the time of a police stop can significantly distort test results. However, with some products the distorted result is significantly reduced 10-20 minutes after ingestion.

Dentures. Surprisingly enough, chemical breath tests should not be given to persons wearing dentures. The officer should request denture removal prior to testing because alcohol could remain lodged in the cracks and emanating vapors can distort test results.

Body Temperature.   A person's body temperature can influence chemical test results. As a general rule, for every two degree increase in body temperature, the chemical breath test registers a 7% higher BAC level. The distortion is greater if the mouth has a high humidity level that often accompanies a fever.

Breathing Patterns.   Breathing patterns influence chemical breath test results.   Holding your breath for 30 seconds before submitting to a breath test will increase BAC results by 15%. Normal breathing with the mouth closed for five minutes will increase results by 7%.   And hyperventilation decreases the test result by 10%. *Strategy:* Attempt to increase oxygen intake prior to giving a breath sample.   Never leave your mouth closed for several minutes, and inhale most of the air through your *mouth*.

Accurate Sample.   Always request a clean mouthpiece before each test. Alcohol vapors can remain trapped in the mouthpiece and cause a higher BAC result. The "clean" air may contain alcohol vapor from the previous person tested on the machine, so the result could contain your breath, plus the other suspect's, causing an inflated BAC result. If the officer fails to run clean air through the machine and administer a blank test prior to your sample, the result may be held inadmissible.

Acetaldehyde.   Oral contraceptives contain acetaldehyde, and pregnant women have higher levels of the chemical in their bodies.

This is significant because acetaldehyde is often detected by chemical tests as ethanol, and therefore presents a false BAC result.

Physiological Factors. Some individuals manufacture alcohol internally, so they can register positive BAC levels without consuming alcohol. This can skew chemical test results, when in fact, the person did not consume enough alcohol to be considered legally intoxicated.

Radio Wave Interference. Another influential factor is radio wave interference. There are numerous sources--AM/FM radios, hand-held walkie-talkies, dispatcher transmissions, teletypes, police radar units, and even electrical storms. Each device can distort the chemical breath test results.

Scientific Margin of Error. Chemical testing equipment has an inherent margin of error, roughly 5%. The standard margin of error has been incorporated into some state laws to avoid judicial dismissals based upon scientific inaccuracies. If a chemical test result is within the margin of error for a specific testing device, it is often inadmissible in a license suspension hearing and criminal trial.

Denial of Independent Testing

An independent chemical test allows the motorist to select a qualified medical professional to administer a BAC analysis that is not sponsored by the government. Most states give motorists the right to demand an independent blood test but only *after* submitting to a chemical test of the officer's choice. The motorist must satisfactorily complete the officer's chemical test to earn the right to an alternate test. If the officer fails to comply with this statutory right, the original chemical test result is often held inadmissible in court.

Naturally, the problem with this statute is the issue of credibility. Most suppression hearings involve conflicting testimony--the defendant versus the officer. In one case, the officer denied an alternate test because the defendant merely *requested* a blood test, rather than *demanding* one, and the judge allowed evidence of the police test result. In another instance, the officer denied that the defendant ever requested a blood test; the judge believed the officer and denied the defendant's motion to suppress the chemical test result.

Involuntary Blood Test

An involuntary blood test is administered when a motorist is either unconscious or otherwise unable to consent to a chemical test. A debate is brewing over the legal authority of police officers to force motorists into providing a blood sample for chemical testing. Surprisingly, courts do not consider blood extraction to be an unreasonably intrusive activity; instead, it is merely physical evidence, like hair and fingerprints, and not testimonial evidence, such as speech. Previously, the courts required that physical evidence be accessible to the public, like signatures, but the most recent cases are further eroding individual constitutional rights. Be sure to have your attorney file a motion to suppress the BAC result from an involuntarily administered chemical test to preserve the issue for appeal.

Controlling BAC Levels

The most distorted belief among jurors involves the legality of drinking and driving. Contrary to popular belief, it is perfectly legal to drink and drive; it only becomes unlawful when drinking impairs individual driving abilities. Thus, it is important to understand alcohol absorption rates so motorists can control and minimize their BAC levels.

Consume Food. There are conflicting sources as to whether it is most beneficial to consume predominantly protein and carbohydrates, as opposed to carbohydrates and fats, prior to consuming alcohol. Regardless of which source is accurate, it is better to eat a balanced meal, rather than specific foods, because a full stomach will reduce the rate of alcohol absorption into the bloodstream.

Best Time to Eat. There is a greater reduction in BAC levels when eating is involved. However, timing is crucial. Eating one-half hour before consuming alcohol has a greater impact on slowing alcohol absorption than a two-hour distance. As the period of time extends beyond two hours, the effect on alcohol absorption decreases; after four hours, previously consumed food has no effect on alcohol absorption. Thus, it is best to continuously snack while drinking, but avoid salty foods--salt promotes the consumption of fluids, which usually contain alcohol.

Nicotine. Studies indicate that nicotine slows alcohol absorption, so smokers have a distinct advantage over nonsmokers, at least in this respect.

Zinc. Alcohol metabolism is affected by the intake of zinc. Higher zinc levels in the body result in slower alcohol metabolism rates; conversely, alcohol metabolizes faster in persons with zinc deficiencies.

Test Result vs. Test Refusal

The foregoing discussion illustrates that it is very difficult to convict motorists of drunk driving when the prosecution lacks sufficient evidence of intoxication. By minimizing the incriminating information that is given to an officer, the opportunity for acquittal significantly increases. Naturally, there are consequences for every course of action, so understand the advantages and disadvantages of each option before making a final decision.

Test Refusal. The denial of all testing--field sobriety, PBT and chemical--will offer the best advantage at a criminal trial. The likelihood of a criminal conviction is diminished, so the defendant can avoid most of the severe punishment--hefty fines, jail, probation, and higher insurance costs. A drunk driving conviction can affect employment options, especially for persons with commercial and chauffeur licenses, and increases the chance for a second offense. Since the conviction can hang over your head for up to 15 years, even the most cautious person has a greater likelihood of another arrest; one mistake at age 21 can haunt a person well into their thirties, potentially devastating a stable family and career.

On the other hand, refusing a chemical test has stern consequences to driving privileges, and may affect the criminal punishment. There is often a lengthier suspension period, and a conviction can have a somewhat longer jail sentence or higher fine. Although the defendant can challenge the legitimacy of the suspension because the arresting officer lacks hard evidence of intoxication, in most instances the department of transportation will uphold the sanction.

Consenting to Field Sobriety Tests.   Naturally, as the number of failed sobriety tests increases, the ability to create reasonable doubt in the jurors' minds decreases. Although the field sobriety tests are subject to effective rebuttal, and the PBT result is inadmissible in a criminal trial, the opportunity for acquittal decreases because there is more incriminating evidence. However, consenting to these field sobriety tests is not nearly as devastating as a chemical test result.

Test Result.   In most drunk driving cases, a chemical test result is the proverbial final nail in the coffin. If the test result is too high, few medical experts can justify the margin of error, and even fewer jurors will acquit. It is only when the test result is closer to the legal limit that expert testimony will be crucial.

Another drawback to providing a chemical test is the expense. A test result near or above the legal limit will inevitably prompt a criminal charge, and exorbitant legal defense fees. To present the best defense and maximize the chance of acquittal, medical and scientific expert testimony is imperative. This can cost thousands of dollars, not to mention attorney fees, deposition costs, and other expenses. Of course, you can reduce legal fees by eliminating expert testimony, but this also reduces the likelihood of an acquittal. Money buys justice, so consider the degree of risk you are willing to assume. *Strategy:* Legal fees are substantially less when the defendant refuses to submit to a chemical test or declines the field sobriety tests. The cost gradually increases with each sobriety test that is performed.

Finally, few motorists realize that drunk driving charges can be filed even though the BAC result is *below* the legal limit. Most statutes allow drunk driving prosecutions if the driver is impaired to *any* extent. Thus, providing a chemical test is no guarantee against a drunk driving charge or criminal conviction.

Taking the Test: Factors to Consider

Always contemplate your options prior to drinking; never make a rash decision during the frantic moments of a police stop. If you are unsure of your estimated BAC, there are several available options.

Use logic and reason to guide your conduct, otherwise a hasty decision can have long-term consequences.

Self-Assessment. There are numerous factors to weigh at the time of a police stop, but the most important consideration is a self-assessment of your condition. In other words, try to reconstruct the evening to assess the food eaten, amount and type of alcohol consumed, medications or drugs ingested, and other factors that influence alcohol absorption. It is beneficial to memorize Charts 2 and 3 to quickly estimate BAC levels. Most people find it useful to multiply the estimated number of drinks by 1.5 to err on the side of caution.

A self-assessment can be used to determine the level of cooperation with police testing. If your estimated impairment is below the legal limit for BAC results, then performing field sobriety tests and consenting to a PBT and chemical test may be warranted. However, if you are driving drunk, then it is best to protect your rights by refusing all police testing. Performing tests could be detrimental to the amount of substance abuse treatment required or criminal punishment imposed.

Know Your Priorities. If there is serious concern about spending a night in jail, then some level of cooperation may be appropriate. However, this has a consequence. If you provide too much information, not only will an arrest occur, but a conviction is often inevitable. Only in rare instances is it possible to talk your way out of a drunk driving arrest. Police officers have a legal obligation to arrest persons when there is probable cause of criminal conduct. Since society has such a negative perception of drinking and driving, talking only provides the officer with more evidence of intoxication. Remain silent, and let your lawyer do the talking.

Cost of Legal Defense. It is very expensive to properly defend a drunk driving case, but this must be weighed against future costs associated with a drunk driving conviction--higher insurance rates, hefty fines, court costs, ignition interlock device, vehicle impoundment, license reinstatement fees, jail sentence, probation, substance abuse treatment, and the possibility of a future drunk driving offense (with enhanced criminal penalties and civil sanctions). Consider all the ramifications, the financial feasibility of asserting a complete legal defense, and other important factors that must be weighed when deciding to protect your constitutional rights.

Although few members of the legal profession will admit that money buys justice, it is a cruel fact of life. Spending more money on criminal defense translates into a greater opportunity for acquittal. It is no surprise that celebrities often win acquittals while the poor are often convicted. Thoroughly analyze your financial resources--liquid assets, equity, collateral, or loan capabilities--to determine the amount you are willing to commit toward a drunk driving defense.

Witnesses. When deciding whether to submit to a chemical test, consider the number of witnesses available to testify on your behalf. If there are passengers in the vehicle, it can be advantageous to perform field sobriety tests because witness testimony can rebut the officer's observations. The only concern is whether the passengers observe the tests and whether their testimony will benefit the defense. This can be a gamble, but it is worth considering at the time of a police stop.

Reason for the Police Stop. Another factor in the decision to perform field sobriety tests is the reason for the police stop. If the officer claims you were weaving or straddling the lane, then it may be best to forego all testing to minimize the negative evidence of intoxication. However, if the reason for the police stop is speeding or driving without headlights, then compliance is more acceptable because such innocuous offenses have little correlation to intoxicated driving. Be cautious. The fact that field sobriety tests are requested indicates that the officer suspects the motorist of drunk driving. If there was an accident, then it is usually advantageous to abstain from any testing procedures.

PBT Result. When in doubt, some defendants consent to the PBT. The device, either hand-held or mounted in a squad car, offers some guidance on how to proceed. If the result is close to the legal limit, then a chemical test remains a viable option; a high BAC result is a warning not to provide a chemical test at the station. Unfortunately, this course of action can have a potentially harsher criminal penalty with a subsequent guilty plea or conviction. Even though the PBT is inadmissible at trial, the result is available to the prosecuting attorney, judge, defense attorney and department of transportation. Moreover, the officer is not obligated to reveal the PBT result, so the motorist must risk that the officer will not exaggerate the BAC level.

There is at least one advantage to refusing a PBT test. A refusal is not admissible at trial. Since the PBT is unreliable and scientifically inaccurate, this evidence is withheld from juror consideration.

8

Pending Charges

Whether or not a chemical test is administered, in most instances the motorist will be arrested. At the police station, the defendant is fingerprinted, booked, given a standard-issue jumpsuit, and placed in a cell until the initial appearance (usually in the morning). The purpose of an initial appearance is to notify the defendant of all charges, and either set bond or order release from jail without bond. In some instances, instead of spending a night in jail the officer imposes a standard bond fee that allows the motorist to be released. This is a discretionary action on the part of the officer, typically contingent upon jail overcrowding, defendant cooperation, and the officer's disposition. If released, a future court date is set for the initial appearance.

Generally, a drunk driving arrest is merely a complaint alleging that criminal activity has occurred; it is not a formal criminal charge. The charge becomes formal upon indictment or the prosecuting attorney filing appropriate papers. There are deadlines for filing formal charges, and only in rare circumstances is the complaint dismissed. There is often a delay between arrest and indictment so the officer can prepare an official police report to factually substantiate the criminal complaint. This also allows the defendant time to retain an attorney.

License Suspension Hearing

Frequently, motorists have the right to a hearing to challenge the legitimacy of a driver's license suspension. Although an attorney is not required, and often cannot prevent a license suspension, it is often wise to request a hearing and have an attorney present. Not only can it function as an inexpensive deposition for the criminal charge, it provides valuable insight into the strengths and weaknesses of your case before the prosecuting attorney has time to prepare. The state is often represented by a law school intern who has little or no legal training or experience. Shrewd defense lawyers can uncover crucial facts to bolster their case for a criminal trial.

Since the driver's license suspension hearing is often tape recorded, defense counsel can obtain a copy of the record for future litigation. The transcript is useful for investigating the case, preparing for depositions, or discrediting the officer's testimony at trial. Catching an officer in a lie or highlighting contradictions in their testimony is powerful and persuasive evidence that often sways a jury to acquit rather than convict.

Substance Abuse Evaluation

As part of the initial appearance, the judge typically orders a substance abuse evaluation to determine whether the defendant has a drinking problem. Unfortunately, this seemingly innocuous report will heavily influence the prosecutor's recommendation and judge's sentence. Since the evaluation plays such a critical role in the punishment portion of a drunk driving charge, defendants should approach it with the same degree of seriousness.

Advance Preparation. Before speaking with a counselor, every defendant should contemplate answers to common substance abuse questions. Most counselors follow a standard questionnaire to evaluate substance abuse problems. Each answer is scored, and the cumulative sum is compared to a chart that recommends a wide range of treatments. Properly prepared defendants will have a lower score and less recommended substance abuse treatment, whereas the ill-prepared may be characterized as chronic substance abusers who need extensive, prolonged and expensive treatment.

Standard Questions. Counselors are searching for answers that reflect a substance abuse problem. Here is a list of typical standardized questions used by counselors. Carefully review, and contemplate your response prior to undergoing a substance abuse evaluation.

1. Do you binge drink (4 drinks or more in one sitting)?
2. Do you drink alone?
3. Do you only drink on special occasions (holidays, weddings, birthdays)?
4. Have you ever experienced blackouts (lost memory from the night before)?
5. Does your family have a history of alcoholism?
6. At what age did you begin consuming alcohol?
7. How often do you consume alcohol?
8. Have you ever used illegal substances?
9. Do you have any prior alcohol-related offenses?
10. Have you had prior substance abuse treatment?

Obviously, common sense can properly answer these questions to avoid the appearance of having a substance abuse problem. Here is one client's response:

1. Never binge drinks.
2. Never drinks alone.
3. Does not usually drink on special occasions.
4. Never experienced blackouts.
5. No family history of alcoholism.
6. 21.
7. 2-3 times per month.
8. No illegal substances used.
9. No prior alcohol-related offenses.
10. No prior substance abuse treatment.

These answers indicate the defendant does not have a substance abuse problem.

Dishonest Evaluation. Some defendants are concerned that dishonest responses can be verified through public records. Although substance abuse evaluations are confidential, that does not prevent the evaluating institution from utilizing its past records to find inconsistencies. Thus, if the defendant had prior substance abuse treatment with the same counselor or institution, or previously revealed a history of problems, then these records will be considered. An untruthful defendant could be caught in a lie, which may lead to contempt of court or additional criminal charges.

Proving Deception. It may be impossible to prove deception on questions 1-8, though records may exist on questions 5, 6, 8-10. It is important to consider whether this information is available to others before answering the questions. Typically, counselors will not search public records for contradictory evidence; instead, it is the prosecutor or judge that may discover this information. For instance, if the defendant had three prior drunk driving convictions, and the counselor only recommends minimum treatment, then the prosecutor and judge will realize the defendant lied on the evaluation.

In one case, the defendant had prior drunk driving convictions in two different states. The prosecutor was unaware of these prior offenses, so the defendant was charged with first offense drunk driving. The defendant immediately pled guilty to the offense before the prosecutor could discover the prior convictions. He delayed the substance abuse evaluation until his criminal and driving records were obtained from the prosecution. Once it was confirmed that the prosecutor did not know of the prior offenses, the defendant lied to the substance abuse counselor to receive the minimum recommended treatment. He deceived everyone, and received the minimum sentence.

In an identical scenario, the defendant was not so lucky. Immediately prior to sentencing, his embittered ex-wife provided the prosecutor with documentation to prove there were prior drunk driving convictions. Naturally, the prosecutor filed contempt charges and the defendant received ten days in jail. On the upside, had the defendant been truthful, he would have been convicted of third offense drunk driving, and received five years in prison.

Risk/Benefit Analysis. Every lie entails a certain amount of risk. As a lawyer, I cannot condone lying, but it happens every day. Some clients lie to their attorney, others to judges, and still others to counselors. The previous examples illustrate the negative consequences of lying, such as additional punishment; however, in many instances the punishment is less severe, so this inevitably promotes dishonesty. Before deciding to lie, it is essential to consider the benefits and consequences of your actions.

Confidentiality. An important consideration is the issue of counselor-client confidentiality. The evaluation is confidential, so defendants should only authorize its release to defense counsel. Since substance abuse evaluations are subjective, an adverse recommendation could result in a harsher criminal sentence. By only authorizing the release of information to an attorney, the defendant retains the option of selecting a different counselor to obtain a more accurate evaluation. If the evaluation is reasonable, then the defendant can authorize the counselor to release information to the prosecuting attorney and court officials.

By shopping for the best evaluation, the defendant is assured a more lenient sentence. Conversely, accepting one evaluation places the defendant at the mercy of a potentially fanatical counselor who classifies any alcohol use as a substance abuse problem. The defendant should treat the substance abuse evaluation with the same level of seriousness as a second medical opinion.

Money Wins Cases

It should come as no surprise that money is a vital factor to winning a high percentage of drunk driving cases. Large financial reserves allow defense attorneys to pursue all avenues of investigation, discovery and legal representation. Indigents suffer the worst injustices because court-appointed attorneys are not allowed to provide equal justice to everyone. Although judges and prosecutors claim there are no limitations when representing the poor, they fail to reveal that court-appointed attorneys are often denied fees if they spend too much time pursuing justice. In addition, most public defenders are overworked, so they lack adequate time to litigate every possible issue.

Hiring a private attorney has the same effect. If the defendant has financial limitations, then there will be limits to the level of justice received. Inevitably, the wealthy are acquitted, or the charges are reduced or dropped. The reason for this is clear: wealthy individuals have the advantage of deposing every conceivable witness, challenging the chain of custody for all evidence, including chemical specimens, performing independent testing of all chemical evidence, researching all possible legal issues, filing countless motions to suppress evidence or dismiss the charges, hiring investigators to find potential witnesses to corroborate the defendant's testimony, investigating the background of the arresting officer(s) to discover impeachable evidence, researching prior arrests to show officer prejudice, etc. An intensive investigation and vigorous defense ultimately casts doubt on the merits of the prosecution's case, which inevitably results in a dismissal or acquittal.

Unfortunately, most defendants do not have the financial resources to undertake such a thorough legal defense, so corners must be cut to reduce legal fees. Each dollar removed from the attorney's pocket places the defendant four quarters closer to a conviction. If a public defender had represented O.J. Simpson, the trial would have lasted two weeks, and he would be on death row. Instead, he hired the best legal defense that money could buy, employed a massive team to investigate the case, raised every conceivable legal issue, and extended the trial for nearly a year. The result: an acquittal.

The key to winning drunk driving cases is information. It is not necessary to twist testimony into a pretzel or establish the officer is lying, nor is it essential to have verifiable proof of sobriety. The defense attorney does not have to argue that the drunk driving laws should be abolished, or that chemical testing is wholly inaccurate. The goal is to provide competent, credible information so the jury can see both sides of the story--often two believable versions--yet feel compelled to vote for an acquittal because reasonable doubt was created through conflicting evidence.

9

Preventive Medicine

Since an accusation of drunk driving is virtually inevitable at some point in your life, the first step is minimizing the factors that trigger drunk driving arrests. Of course, abstinence is the best way to prevent an arrest, but this is often impractical. Most people are social drinkers, and it is perfectly legal to drink and drive. If you are drinking alcohol, even socially, then you are susceptible to a drunk driving arrest. Therefore, it is essential to know your rights before operating a motor vehicle.

Preventing a Police Stop

The best way to reduce the chance of a drunk driving arrest is preventing the initial police stop. First and foremost, be familiar with the vehicle you are driving. Many arrests are precipitated by erratic driving behavior due to the motorist's unfamiliarity with the car. The person is often driving a friend's car, and the irregular driving involves: 1) searching for dashboard switches; 2) stopping too quickly because of unfamiliarity with the brake sensitivity; or 3) driving a manual transmission when they are more familiar with an automatic, or vice versa.

The key is taking precautions before driving. The ability to correct minor driving irregularities, which are often unrelated to alcohol impairment, can reduce the chance of being stopped by the police. Regardless of the excuse used for driving erratically, this creates probable cause to justify a police stop, which allows the officer to inquire about the driver's consumption of alcohol. Consequently, it is imperative to act responsibly before driving so you can prevent a police stop.

Vehicle Contents

Prior to any police stop, every motorist should stock their vehicle with several essential items. Each component is intended to reduce the indicators of intoxication that officers rely upon to substantiate a drunk driving arrest. Since most drunk driving arrests are precipitated by the officer's initial contact with the driver, it is essential to use this opportunity to present yourself in a non-incriminating manner. In other words, motorists must take precautions to disguise the indicators of intoxication to avoid being wrongfully charged with a drunk driving offense.

Cologne or Perfume. Always stock the vehicle with a strong cologne or perfume. Use expensive brands because they often have stronger scents that last longer. Cheap brands decline in performance shortly after application. Use a small bottle, preferably with a spray applicator, so it can be easily placed in a vehicle storage compartment.

The purpose of cologne or perfume is to mask the smell of alcoholic beverages. Although alcohol has no odor, officers often testify that the beverage flavoring is a strong indicator of intoxication. Since non-alcoholic beer contains an odor of alcohol, a sober person could be falsely accused of drunk driving. Apply the fragrance to the torso region, face (near the mouth), wrist or hands, and lightly to the hair. This creates an alternative aroma in the bodily regions that are most accessible to the officer during questioning at the scene of a police stop.

Breath-Enhancing Products. Another essential item for the vehicle is a breath-enhancing product. Be selective in the purchase, and experiment in advance to determine which product works best for you. The type of breath freshener is important. Do not sacrifice quality to save a few pennies. Purchase candy or chewing gum with a strong pungency, red-hot cinnamon, or other breath-enhancing products, like Nu-Breath®.

Breath-enhancing products not only mask the odor of alcohol, but also offer an explanation when the officer alleges that the driver had slurred speech. Inevitably, a person eating candy will not be articulate. Thus, breath fresheners eliminate another subjective indicator of intoxication, and help protect the motorist against false accusations of drunk driving.

Air Freshener. Always have a supply of air freshener in the vehicle to disguise the odor of alcohol that emanates from the interior. When an officer approaches, the first indicator of intoxication is the aroma of the vehicle's interior. This inevitably prompts questioning about whether the driver consumed alcohol. A spray canister is preferable to an air freshener dangling from the rearview mirror.

Reserve Supply. Always maintain a reserve supply to prevent an incident where there is a shortage of essential items. Check the vehicle contents before drinking to eliminate performing this task *after* a night of drinking.

Cumulative Benefit. By using cologne and perfume in conjunction with breath fresheners, the odor of alcohol becomes a figment of the officer's imagination. Naturally, this will not prevent a dishonest officer from lying, but it is strong evidence to cast doubt on their testimony.

When to Use the Products

The body fragrance, breath deodorizer, and air freshener should be used prior to the officer approaching the vehicle. Usually, an initial police stop allows the driver 30 seconds to several minutes before the officer approaches the vehicle. The police typically contact the dispatcher to confirm their location and run the license plate search to verify owner registration. Other times, the officer will promptly approach the driver to obtain a driver's license, and then return to the squad car to check its validity. *Strategy:* Prior to driving, anticipate a possible police stop. Freshen the car's interior and your appearance. This will give the products sufficient time to disguise the odor of alcohol, and provides the driver with a sense of security.

Regardless of the approach, it is imperative that the motorist act promptly to avoid being wrongfully charged. Zealous officers can fabricate evidence of intoxication, so using the products will protect your constitutional rights and provide greater ammunition to expose the officer's deceitfulness. If the ingredients are properly used, you may be able to prevent a driver's license suspension. Since the products offer a legitimate explanation to the so-called "indicators of intoxication," it casts doubt on whether the officer had probable cause for a drunk driving charge.

Content Location. Always have the essential vehicle contents easily accessible to the driver. If the officer notices the driver leaning toward the glove compartment or searching under the seat, it will look suspicious and the officer may suspect a weapon or illegal contraband in the vehicle. Place the items in an accessible location--center console, dashboard ledge, or tape deck storage compartment--to avoid appearing suspicious. This allows immediate access, quick application, and additional time for the products to conceal the odor of alcohol.

Consider Options Beforehand. Absent field sobriety tests, motorists are in the best position to defend against a drunk driving charge. But this decision should be made before the initial police stop and arrest. Each circumstance is different so be mindful that in some instances cooperation is the best medicine. If your self-assessment indicates that compliance is appropriate, then trust your judgment, but also be prepared to spend an evening in jail. Compliance usually results in an arrest. On the other hand, noncompliance will often have the same repercussions.

Furthermore, contemplate the impact on your driving privileges. A chemical test refusal has a lengthier license suspension. Although the suspension can be challenged, it is usually upheld. Thus, it is important to understand the added inconvenience of a test refusal-- lengthier driver's license suspension, requirements for a temporary permit, higher insurance rates, and possibly an ignition interlock device.

Although many drivers still operate vehicles without a temporary permit, the consequences of a drunk driving charge can be more severe if you are arrested for driving under suspension. This can impact the plea agreement, sentencing options, and punishment imposed. Think twice before resorting to this route.

Avoid Self-Incrimination. The most important rule of thumb is never attempt to talk your way out of an arrest. The more you say, the more likely you will be charged and convicted of drunk driving. Speaking to the officer provides the prosecution with incriminating information that will be used against you in a court of law.

The same advice applies to field sobriety tests. If the tests are properly performed, the officer can still claim the results indicate a test failure, regardless of the defendant's perception of success. Moreover, the jury is more likely to believe a sober officer, than a motorist who admitted to drinking and failed sobriety tests. Since drinking can impair a person's judgment, the defendant's recollection of passing the field sobriety tests is likely to be viewed as erroneous because their cognitive abilities were diminished.

Finally, the refusal to perform tests should continue at the police station. Often officers will request voluntary compliance in answering a standardized questionnaire. The questions are designed to assess your impairment, and can be used against you at trial. By voluntarily supplying incriminating information, you limit the chance of an acquittal.

Appendix A

GLOSSARY

actual possession: The immediate occupancy or direct physical control over an object.

administrative law judge: Person presiding over an administrative hearing with the power to administer oaths, take testimony, rule on evidentiary matters, and make determinations of factual issues.

black-and-white fever: A nervous condition that frequently occurs in motorists who have been followed by the police for a lengthy period of time, causing them to drive erratically because they are concentrating on their rearview mirror instead of the road.

constructive possession: Possession that is assumed to exist, where the person has sufficient, though not actual, physical control over the object.

controlled substance: Any drug specifically designated by the government as narcotic, or other chemicals that are illegal without a prescription.

conviction: A public record that certifies personal responsibility for a crime. A conviction occurs with a guilty verdict, plea of guilty or no contest plea. Regardless of the legal distinctions, in the eyes of the law, each is treated as a conviction. The only exception is the granting of a deferred judgment or other official act that expunges the criminal record or renders the final judgment void.

deferred judgment: When a conviction is removed from the defendant's criminal record after successfully completing a probationary term. There is usually no imprisonment or fine.

deferred sentence: The criminal sentence is postponed, usually until the defendant fulfills certain obligations imposed by the court. It is not the same as a suspended sentence.

divided-attention tests: Field sobriety tests that require the defendant to perform tasks requiring simultaneous mental and physical activities, such as the one-leg lift or walk-the-line test.

driver's license suspension: The length of time a motorist is denied the privilege of lawfully driving. *See* Note at end of glossary.

field sobriety tests: A procedure used by law enforcement personnel to determine the alcohol impairment of drivers. There are three standardized tests, which range from physical coordination and verbal articulation to divided-attention activities and involuntary responses.

hard suspension: The length of time a driver's license is suspended where a motorist is not entitled to drive or receive a temporary restricted license.

horizontal gaze nystagmus (HGN): A standardized field sobriety test that monitors the involuntary jerking of the eyes. An object is placed six inches from the eyes and slowly moved in various directions until reaching a 45-degree angle.

implied consent: A statutory requirement in the drunk driving laws that obligates motorists, who operate a motor vehicle within the state, to provide a chemical specimen to measure BAC levels. The law imposes a driver's license sanction for a chemical test failure or refusal.

initial appearance: Usually the first court appearance where the defendant is advised of the alleged criminal charges and constitutional rights. Bail/bond is set, conditions of release are established, and a preliminary hearing date is scheduled.

joint civil liability: Where all the parties are subject to civil liability for the same debt; if one or more person cannot afford the debt, the other(s) must pay that share.

license suspension: *see* driver's license suspension.

Miranda advisement (Miranda rights): The fifth amendment constitutional right against self-incrimination, having an attorney present, or receiving a court-appointed attorney. Police officers must advise defendants of these rights at the time of arrest. If a defendant is taken into custody or experiences a significant deprivation of freedoms and no waiver of rights is provided, all subsequent admissions are inadmissible at trial.

preliminary hearing: A hearing where a judge determines whether there is probable cause that the defendant committed the crime as charged.

reality-based substance abuse education program: Supervised tours of hospitals, treatment facilities or morgues to illustrate the consequences of drunk driving.

suspended sentence: A formal sentence where the judge reduces or eliminates the period of incarceration, provided the defendant successfully completes a probationary period.

suspension: *see* driver's license suspension.

temporary restricted license: A driving permit that authorizes a motorist to operate a motor vehicle despite their driving privileges being suspended, but it only allows traveling to specified places, such as maintaining employment or continuing health care. A TRL cannot be used for pleasure driving.

white-line fever: A condition that frequently occurs after driving a lengthy period of time where the driver becomes hypnotized by the road and often weaves within the traffic lane.

work permit *see* temporary restricted license.

zero tolerance: Underage motorist with a BAC often ranging between .02% and .10%. Adopted by state legislatures as a measure to curb underage drinking and driving.

Note: For purposes of this book, the terms relating to a driver's license suspension will encompass every status of a person's driving privileges, whether suspended, revoked, denied or barred.

Appendix B

ABBREVIATIONS

ALJ: administrative law judge

BAC: blood-alcohol concentration

FST: field sobriety test

HGN: horizontal gaze nystagmus

IID: ignition interlock device

NHTSA: National Highway Traffic Safety Administration

PBT: preliminary breath test

TRL: temporary restricted license (often referred to as a work permit)

INDEX